Child in BLOOM

PRACTICAL ADVICE *for* PARENTING THROUGH *the* GROWING YEARS

RENEE MATTSON, Ph.D.

wellspring

PUBLISHED BY WELLSPRING
AN IMPRINT OF VIIDENT

ISBN: 978-1-63582-570-1 (hardcover)
ISBN: 978-1-63582-571-8 (eBook)

Design by Todd Detering

10 9 8 7 6 5 4 3 2 1

Printed in the United States of America

Table of Contents

Part One · INTRODUCTION

Part Two · CONNECTION

Part Three · PARENTING STYLES

Part Four · PARENTING BLISS

Part Five · TOP TIPS

Part Six · **CLOSING IT UP**

Part One

Introduction

CHILD IN BLOOM

You and your child are in process and not done yet, so don't give in or give up!

What does it mean to be a **Child in Bloom**? The key word is not "child" or "bloom." The key word is:

"In"—to be standing in the middle of something.

What is it that our children are standing in the middle of? You might say the terrible twos, or the anxious tweens, or maybe the smart-mouthed teens. Wherever your child is developmentally, they are right in the middle of their growing years. The years filled with lots of ups and downs, drama, emotions, behaviors, trials, and more than anything, joy and amazement at the learning and growth that is happening right before our very eyes.

Sometimes the best vantage point for seeing this growth is from a bird's eye view. Try to fly high above the emotion, the clutter, and the fatigue of raising kids and see what's really going on.

I am a parent coach, and it is my job to sit side by side with parents to help them see what is right in front of them. They are caught up in the craziness of their day-to-day lives and I get to help them pause and check in to see where they are and where they want to be as a family. They are usually already doing things that are terrific, and if there is a sticky situation, they usually just need a little knowledge and tools to help them get through it. Because it is difficult for me to sit side by side with everyone who needs this kind of perspective, I hope that by writing this book and sharing the ideas within it, I will be able to help you see more clearly what is going on in your home, and how you can make things start to shift in the right direction.

So many parents I meet with feel stuck in a rut and they are finding it hard to move beyond it. I like to help them see they are not stuck; they are simply in the middle of a growing process that has a beginning, an end, and steps between here and there. The good news is all children have the potential to change and discover new ways to deal with their world, and you as their parent have the power to support this change.

I call this my In Bloom theory. When you are standing in the middle of something, it can be very difficult to see what's happening. But something really is happening, something with a beginning, an end, and a long process between here and there.

No matter how old a child is, they are right in the middle of growing. That makes your child a **Child in Bloom**, with potential to change and discover new ways to deal with their world.

We can take this theory beyond our kids to the rest of our world. We can be:

Parents in Bloom. We are right in the middle of growing as parents, constantly changing and adding skills to our toolbox.

Families in Bloom. As a group, we are evolving and will continue to do so from start to finish. Is there ever really a finish to a family? I don't think so. Families go on and on, and generations endlessly affect each other.

Heck, we can even say **Friends in Bloom, Teachers in Bloom, Doctors in Bloom,** or **Bankers in Bloom.** Whoever you are and whatever you are in the middle of is a part of the process of your life.

I say "process, not product" on purpose. You are not supposed to be a finished product; perfect and pristine and ready to box up and sell. You are in motion and ever-changing as you experience the world around you and alter your perspective and skills to survive. You really are growing and because you are right in the middle of it, it can be very difficult to see the bits of progress.

Here's the sticky part. The family, the parent, and the child are all constantly **in MOTION.** Yet no one has paused to recognize that it is simply part of the process. So keep moving. Don't get stuck. Try something new that you find in this book or another helpful resource for parenting.

Don't fixate on the problem behavior. Instead, find and try new solutions. Recognize the smallest moments of positive growth that can help you move your child up to the next level of their development.

ACTION STEP: So from here forward, no more fixating, no more stuck in a rut. It is time to make a change and time to see the growth potential for you and your child.

PRAY FOR YOUR PARENTING WITH PAUSE, PATTERN, AND PURPOSE

Parenting can be stressful and channeling prayer can only help.

The day you drop them off to spend time with the new sitter.
Your child's first ride on a school bus.
A sleepover at their friend's house.
Waiting test results when their fever is high.
Hoping they made the team.

As parents, we experience every emotion as our children go through the regular trials of their life. During these times, their worry and strife become our own. We could dwell here in the worry zone, trying to control the scene and make everything just right, or we could let go and let God.

When my three kids were young, and even to this day, I was lucky to have a mentor in parenting whose boys were about ten years ahead of my kids. She had walked through these worries before me, and I watched her come out on the other side worry-free.

I asked her one day how she did it without going crazy and locking the boys up, never to see the light of day, in order to protect them from the snares of the world. She knew it was tempting to hold them tight, but she also knew they were not hers to hold back. She reminded me of the power of prayer.

She simply said, "I cannot protect them on my own and cannot hold them back from experiencing the world outside our home." She went on to tell me how she started a daily prayer ritual. What made it a ritual was the fact that it was sacred and she allowed it to pause the day. This ritual had pattern. She prayed in the same place, in the same way, and tried to do it every day and on purpose, especially when the worries were getting the best of her. It was her sacred place to go and rest when she was worn down by parenting worries.

One of her three main worries was the boys' physical safety (as they headed out to practice, games, and new driving experiences that inevitably put them in harm's way, far from her watch). She also prayed for their security and protection from callous people in situations that could possibly hurt their hearts and confidence. And finally, she prayed for their purity of soul. These prayers were sent forth to keep them clean and clear of the corrupted world outside their door.

Three simple prayers to rest her worries upon. **SAFETY, SECURITY,** and **PURITY.** She knew this was all she could do beyond her focused parenting approaches. The rest would have to be up to God.

Her words hit home for me. I'm confident they came straight from God because they came right at a time when worry was overtaking my day. I was spending so much time worrying as a new parent. My mom had called it raising kids in the "Age of Anxiety" where all the information coming at us made everything from peanut butter to car seat buckles potential threats to my child's life.

All that time worrying, but I wasn't purposely praying with pause and pattern. So from that day forward, I added prayers for my kids to my morning routine.

The squares of my shower became sacred in that they served as space for me to place each worry for each child in a separate square during my daily shower. I zeroed in on the prayer format for safety, security, and purity. I added specific requests for each of our kids' daily needs and a touch of gratitude for their successes and growth.

Since then, I've done this practice every day. To think of all the daily prayers I have sent forth from these shower squares. Every little daily worry was able to rest on God. This practice provided me with solace and understanding as I realized I cannot do it all, and worrying does nothing to help the situation. To let go is to let God.

Like St. Therese of Lisieux, who added prayer to the little moments of her life, I began to add prayer to the small and natural moments within my day. I prayed for my children while watering the flowers. I prayed for my family while washing the dishes. I prayed for my husband's work while taking a walk, and I prayed for my neighbor as I passed them by on the street. An abundance of prayers has led to an abundance of grace. Let go and let God give you this kind of abundance.

ACTION STEP: Read Psalm 91 and begin to rely on God as your family and children's protector. Then pause to read about St. Therese of Lisieux and try her practice of praying through the little moments, whether they be sacred squares in your shower or each weed you pull from a garden. Make your prayers purposeful, patterned, and pause your day to make sure they happen. You will be amazed at the outcome.

Part Two

Connection

BUT FIRST, CONNECT

Take time today to pause into your parenting and connect with your kids.

Wouldn't it be lovely to pick up a parenting book and on the first page find the secret to raising great kids? What if you found out that you already have the secret? What if I told you the secret is instinctual, but the signals get confused by all the outside noise and busyness coming your way?

During the early days of your parenting, you carved out time to get to know your child. Throughout this time, you acted automatically. You stared at them all day long, eyes locked on the child before you. Every little noise they made cued you to do the next thing. You felt like you'd known them for a lifetime and you offered them an understanding and forgiveness that comes with a parent's unconditional love. Through all this, you were connected parent-to-child in the most natural bond that came easily, even though you'd never met each other before. Pure connection overshadowed everything.

Fast forward to repeated sleepless nights, toddler tantrums, school-age whining, and teenage rebellion that are also natural parts of the developmental pathway. Along this journey, your parenting situation got a little tougher. You began to replace the pure connection with the busyness of life and all of its expectations. Correction became the norm and connections went to the bottom of the to-do list. Some days there was no time for connection at all.

I don't have to tell you that the parent-child relationship is the most important relationship on the planet. Your gut told you that on day one. It's also the toughest job you will ever have. You knew that on day one, too. Connection is the cornerstone to this relationship and without it, the house will crumble, all the rules you make will falter, and your consequences and follow-through will fade. This is important so listen closely. . .

It's early on in this book and I am going to give you the secret to parenting right away. Here goes. . . **Remember what it felt like on day one of your child's life.**

Slow down like you did back then. Take time to pause so you can pay attention to what your parenting instincts are trying to tell you. But first, connect!

ACTION STEP: Carve out time in your day to pause for parenting. Connect with your parenting and then begin to think about how you can add connection into your relationship with your child. How and when do you connect with your child or children? List all the ways.

BIBLE VERSE: "And whoever receives one child such as this in my name receives me" (Mark 9:37).

CONNECT 4 AND YOU'LL HAVE MORE

Adult-child relationships are the key to changed behavior.

As a parent, you know that time is a true commodity.

You are busy putting order to your family life while putting food on the table. You spend your time making sure your kids read that last book before bed or checking in on their homework. You tell them they did awesome at soccer, you go to parent teacher conferences, among a thousand other things. Isn't all this enough? Of course all these things are necessary parts of this job, but in the midst of these busy parts of your routine, it can be easy to miss out on the slightest moments of connection that signal you were truly present and aware of their presence. You are so busy checking off the next thing that you may not stop to give the thumbs up when you see them make progress, or you may forget to pause a little longer and really hear what they have to say.

When I say connect more, I am talking about slight bits of connection that could easily slip by. These slight connections can take less than a minute, but when done right can last a lifetime. They do not have to be elaborate trips to a child's favorite store. They don't have to involve a huge celebration after a big win. They can be a silent thumbs up from across the room, a pat on the back when you hear kind words, or a sticky note to say you understand what they need.

Research shows that positive adult-child connection can positively influence behavior. This kind of slight and consistent connection can do this four times more than any formalized discipline measures (such as rule setting, doling out consequences, or monitoring their progress).

Here's the key: Connect 4! Connect four times more than you correct. Put four times more energy into connection than all your other parenting efforts, and you are likely to see more positive changes in behavior. **Time on connection is time well spent.** Here are four outcomes of consistently connecting:

1. You get to know your child and their motivations better.
2. You become more aware of how they are growing and progressing.
3. You build a trusting and mutually respectful relationship.
4. You nurture a safe space where the child can return when things inevitably get tough.

In the end, parents save time when they add in these tiny moments of connection because they will need to spend less time correcting negative behaviors. *Connect 4 and you will have more!*

ACTION STEP: Add four more slight connections with your kids. Note what happens next.

RESEARCH CONNECTION: Read Mark and Christine Boynton's book *The Educator's Guide to Preventing and Solving Discipline Problems* and visit www.pbisrewards.com/blog/how-do-i-give-positive-reinforcement/

HIGH FIVE PHRASES

Five simple phrases can ensure your child knows you care.

As an educator or parent, there have been many times in my life when I felt like one child and their negative behaviors were ruling the day. It was exhausting saying, "Stop it," "Quit it," and "Don't do that," time after time without any changes in behavior. In fact, I remember one situation with a child I was working with where I finally said, "I quit the quit its!" After that, I knew I needed to replace my current ways with new responses in order to rebuild that connection and relationship.

I decided to focus on that one child in a different kind of way. I decided to give them a high five every day. Not a high five like you are thinking, but five different slight connections within their day to tell them that I was present and ready to connect with them.

Throughout the day, I challenged myself to say these five things to them at least one time each:

1. I see you.
2. I hear you.
3. I know you.
4. I understand you.

AND

5. I see you.

Notice I didn't say "I like your behavior" because I didn't like their behavior. But I did want to like them, and I needed to do this connection to reorder my thoughts around this child. Here are some examples of these high five statements:

I see you: I see the little things you are doing better every day. I see you frustrated by your schoolwork. I see you being patient even when you are annoyed. You've been seen.

> Kids want to feel like they are not invisible to you; they want to be seen.

I hear you: I hear you and I know you have your own opinion. I hear what you want and need. You've been heard and I am taking note of it.

> Kids want to feel heard and sometimes that is all it takes to stop the behavior. You don't have to agree with them, just make sure they know you've heard them.

I know you: I know you and where you have come from. I know what your life entails and where you hope to go next. I know the barriers and supports you have and need, and I know your whole story.

> Kids want to feel like someone really knows them.

I understand you: I understand you and the situation that you are in. I remember what it might feel like because I have been there before. I can also see it from your perspective and have empathy towards what you might be feeling.

> Kids are begging to be understood by the people who surround them.

AND I like you: I like being near you, hanging out with you, and spending time with you. I enjoy you and want to get to see, hear, know, and understand you more.

> This goes beyond loving your child. This "liking" part is so very crucial to building trust. It goes beyond your unconditional love, which is a given. This is a choice to like them and want to be near them. It means much more than loving them.

In my situation with the child, I simply added these five things in daily and day by day, our relationship and the child's behavior began to change.

ACTION STEP: Add these High Five Phrases to your interactions. See the positive results bloom!

BIBLE VERSE: "I have seen the God who sees me!" (Genesis 16:13).

SIDE BY SIDE

Find time for simple joint experiences where you and your child can be side by side as you connect.

As a child, we used to visit our Grammie and Grampa's cottage in Canada. It was rustic and disconnected from the world. That was part of the charm. Being isolated from the world meant we were more connected as a family. We took long walks on the beach side by side as we tried to make it all the way to "the point." We had drawn-out dinners on the deck, sitting side by side as we watched the sun go down. And at the end of the night, we stood side by side as we washed the dishes the old-fashioned way, working as a team to get it all done—a washer, a rinser, a dryer, and someone to put the dishes away.

These side by side moments were naturally fulfilling because they came from sharing a common experience, and they allowed for more meaningful conversations because we kids didn't feel like we were on the spot with all eyes on us, forced to connect. The pressure of face-to-face was gone and there was no expectation to look someone in the eye, which meant we could be a little more honest about what we thought. I have vivid memories and feelings about these connections with my grandparents, my parents, and my siblings at the cottage that have lasted with me throughout my life.

As a teacher I had side by side connections with my students too. When we would sit beside each other to make a craft, read a book, or work on a writing task, the child seemed to let their guard down and share more stories when I wasn't facing them across the table. The same thing happened when we would take a walk together down the hallway. It was a joint experience and a safe arena to let the truth or opinions run free without judgment. **These are the kind of**

connections we all want with our kids, but how can we carve out time to get them?

In two weeks, our youngest son Peter will be taking his driving test. Gaining his license and independence will make him so happy, and that makes us happy, but to be honest we will also be very sad. The many car rides we gave him allowed us a safe space to connect. Whether it would be a long ride home from a sporting event or a short drive to school every morning, he would be more likely to open up because we weren't face-to-face, ready to critique what he said or give away our true feelings through our facial expressions.

We will need to replace this time with him with something else. Maybe we will begin to go places around our city to sit side by side and watch the sun go down or take long walks side by side after dinner. Or maybe we'll pretend we don't have a dishwasher and each take a turn as the washer, rinser, dryer, and someone to put the dishes all away.

ACTION STEP: Find time to sit, stand, walk, or ride side by side with your child and connect. You do not have to ask a lot of questions, but instead wait for the conversation to unfold. You could be doing something together like serving food at a homeless shelter, pulling weeds in the backyard, taking a long walk or short drive, or simply washing the dishes.

BIBLE VERSE: ". . . standing firm side by side, with one mind struggling together for the faith of the gospel" (Philippians 1:27).

RESOURCE: Visit www.ascd.org/el/articles/the-two-minute-relationship- builder.

7

MILESTONES MATTER

Your child or teen is "in process." They aren't done yet. Connect to where they are.

When you were waiting on your baby's arrival, you most likely read books like *What to Expect When You're Expecting* or you followed apps that helped you track your baby's milestones month by month. Then, once the baby arrived, you may have learned about your baby's exciting next steps through a book or app on the stages of infancy. Once your child started to walk and talk, you got busy and probably stopped reading about development. But the development didn't stop there. The stages may have been less obvious, but the growth kept coming and will continue all the way through their young adult life. Does this parenting job ever end? The milestones and stages vary across several domains: speech and language, cognition, motor planning, social emotional, and even spiritual development.

Through the generations, the world has changed so much for kids. We can all recognize this when we look at ourselves and shake our heads at the things we need to address as parents nowadays. But development is the one steady. Kids and their developmental stages stay the same and we can count on them to come at us like clockwork, or at least in a specific sequence.

Thinking of your child as "in process" or a **Child in Bloom** doesn't mean we excuse behavior that is out of line developmentally. It doesn't mean we should say things like, "Well, he's just in a whiny stage, so we let him whine as much as he needs." Please, I beg you, for everyone's fun and function, help your child figure out that whining doesn't work so we can squelch that whining by the time he gets introduced to his kindergarten teacher.

In other words, we want to strive to help our kids burst through each milestone, coming out on the other side with new skills and acquisitions that help them to function and have fun at the next level. Toting their three-year-old responses along the developmental stepping stones to age ten is no fun for anyone, and twenty-three year olds who fuss like teens don't function so well at their newly acquired jobs. So use the milestones to guide you as you understand them. At the same time, prepare to launch them up the ladder and out of the terrible twos and tiring teens to the next layers of life.

Quick Milestones and Mentions to Help You Along the Way:

Under two: Attachment is the focus. Don't forget to divert and distract.

Two and a half: The age of reason.
They can definitely understand "if_____ then _____." *If you get your shoes on, you can go outside. If you eat your carrots, you can have dessert.* Or my favorite: *nice gets nice and nasty gets nothing.*

Three to five: Pretend play rules.
Use pretend as a help for everything. *Sleeping Beauty needs her rest, Spiderman always helps to put his toys away, Godzilla only roars outside.*

Five to eight: Concrete, rule-oriented, and somewhat anxious.
They just left the pretend zone and the real world can be quite overwhelming, so policing the playground, tattling, and stressing over small things helps them put order to their newfound planet. Reading rules, math rules, and writing rules. They are begging for rules so keep them tight.

Eight to twelve: Metacognition begins.
They can think about their thinking and step outside their world to see it from a different perspective. Reading for understanding, creative endeavors, and social butterflying expand. Use these things to your advantage by writing them notes, sharing influential stories together, and leveraging their drive to be with friends.

Twelve to fourteen: Social life and pressure becomes number one. They are beginning the big breakaway so you suddenly know nothing and they wouldn't be caught dead doing something uncool. Their independence is flourishing and their freedom to choose helps you see a new and beautiful side to them. Give them a little more freedom to choose what they do and step back and let natural consequences teach.

Fourteen to sixteen: Sophisticated morons return. Kind of like the terrible twos, they know just enough to be dangerous but still nothing that will allow them to break away completely—yet! Risk and social exploration climb high, so check in much more than you think. Like two year olds, they say, "Me do it myself," but they really mean, "Help me!"

Sixteen to eighteen: Ready to fly the coop. They begin the great breakaway but at this point they recognize the height of the fall. They look to you more and suddenly you aren't so bad. At this time, try to be present more than ever, even if it seems silly. Things are serious and scary, like they were before they went off to kindergarten, but don't be either serious or scary in your responses to them. Laugh and love them as much as possible before they go out that door and make you proud.

ACTION STEP: Pay attention to what's next by reading up on child development all the way through the teens and early twenties. Notice in advance what's coming your child's way. Do this to make sure you are prepared and ready to look at their behavior and say, "Oh, that makes sense. The book told me this might happen. He's normal, that's what four (or fourteen) year olds do."

RESOURCE: Check out my favorite milestone books:

Highly Recommended Books to Support Your Parenting:

- *Your Child's Growing Mind: Brain Development and Learning From Birth to Adolescence* by Jane M. Healy, PhD

- *The Happiest Toddler on the Block: How to Eliminate Tantrums and Raise a Patient, Respectful and Cooperative One- to Four-Year-Old* by Harvey Karp, MD
- *Ages and Stages: A Parent's Guide to Normal Childhood Development* by Charles E. Schaefer, PhD and Theresa Foy DiGeronimo
- *Between: A Guide for Parents of Eight to Thirteen-Year-Olds* by Sarah Ockwell-Smith
- *The Teenage Brain: A Neuroscientist's Survival Guide to Raising Adolescents and Young Adults* by Frances E. Jensen, MD and Amy Ellis Nutt
- *The Spiritual Child: The New Science on Parenting for Health and Lifelong Thriving* by Lisa Miller, PhD

Books to Support Parenting Tweens and Teens

- *The Available Parent: Expert Advice for Raising Successful and Resilient Teens and Tweens* by John Duffy, PhD
- *From Defiance to Cooperation: Real Solutions for Transforming the Angry, Defiant, Discouraged Child* by John F. Taylor, PhD
- *Building Resilience in Children and Teens: Giving Kids Roots and Wings* by Kenneth R. Ginsburg, MD
- *Why Do They Act That Way? A Survival Guide to the Adolescent Brain for You and Your Teen* by David Walsh, PhD
- *Positive Discipline for Teenagers: Empowering Your Teen and Yourself Through Kind and Firm Parenting* by Jane Nelsen, EdD and Lynn Lott, MA
- *Get Out of My Life, But First Could You Drive Me and Cheryl to the Mall?* by Anthony E. Wolf, PhD
- *Parenting with Love & Logic: Teaching Children Responsibility* by Foster Cline, MD and Jim Fay

REMEDY FOR REGULATION

Remedies for regulation can ensure your whole family gets what they need.

Adults find all kinds of ways to calm down or rev up their body in order to feel regulated or in balance. Sipping on your morning cup of joe and holding it warm between your hands might serve as a way to calm you down while at the same time rev you up for your day. An afternoon call to your best friend where you laugh until you cry might serve as a reboot to your system before an afternoon with a heavy workload. Making time for these calm down or rev up remedies helps you ensure that your day runs smoothly. You wouldn't miss them because you need them.

Your kids need them too, but their needs are unique to them. They also need you wired into their day, paying attention to the signals that note when they need to calm down or when they need a pick-me-up. Instead of waiting until these signals show up, you could plan the calm down and rev up remedies on purpose.

You might already do this. For instance, do you avoid your son's after school meltdown if you remember to pack a crunchy snack in the car? Pack it on purpose!

Does your daughter do better with her siblings on Saturday morning if she first has a little time to sit quietly in her room alone before the day gets hectic? Encourage it!

Each of our own kids had their thing we learned to schedule into our day. We learned by watching what they did to calm down naturally and on their own. When Peter was upset, we'd find him covered by all his stuffed animals on his bed. We started to do this "Burrow with

Buddies" on purpose throughout the day just to ward off the worries. Our other son, Mick, was slow to start in the morning, but we noticed when we played some morning jams he would move at a faster pace. We got him a clock radio tuned to his favorite station. And our daughter Evy used to say, "I run around, Mommy. I run around." This was a cue to us that she needed to get her sillies out or calm down her nerves. And now as a working twentysomething, she still schedules her day around her workout because she knows it helps her function at her very best.

Each person in your family has their thing that helps them. It is your job to look for the clues around these items and then plug them in on purpose to ward off the worries, calm down the brain, or to wake up the system. Adding these items in on purpose can change the whole outcome of your child's day.

ACTION STEP: Make a list of your child's sensory supports that help them calm down or rev up. Make a list of your own sensory supports that make you feel better heading into your day. Devise a plan to add these things into your daily routine.

RESOURCE: If you feel like your child's sensory calm down and rev up needs are wreaking havoc on their function of day-to-day living, connect with an expert, OT, or check out these free resources: https://sensationalbrain.com/free-resources/.

9

A WELL-PLACED YES

Use your child's "big asks" as leverage to maturity.

You hear it all the time. "I want this," "I need that," "Why can't I do this?" "When can I do that?" Your child seems to think that having these things and opportunities will change their whole life. You might be apt to say *NO NO NO* to all these "big asks," and rightfully so. Who wants to raise an entitled kid who gets whatever they ask for? You recognize that giving in to all their earthly desires could create a monster. You could raise them to be someone who can't wait, acts impulsively, and has no patience or perseverance. They simply won't know how or what to do while they hold out and wait for the right time. Kudos for you for listening to your parenting gut on this.

Now, I am going to rock your world a bit. What if I told you to think about this whining for worldly things as an opportunity to hear your child? Remember, kids love to feel like they've been heard. Think of this as an opportunity to see beyond "no" or "yes" or black and white and instead see the grayness within it. Instead of giving a blanket no and getting the continual ask until you say yes, you could drop in a well-placed yes. **A well-placed yes is different from a regular old yes. It comes wrapped in an opportunity to see your child grow.**

Here's an example: Your child asks you to go to the mall with their friends, without you. Yikes, you aren't sure you are ready for this big step and let's be honest, you have no confidence in their ability to do this with grace. You've seen how they act around your house lately, and you know those behaviors could be even worse when surrounded by friends in the mall. But this time, instead of an automatic no, pause, think, and then say yes. Or at least say, "I hear you, and I am thinking about it." Think about how you could use her desire to be a grown-up at the mall to encourage grown-up behavior from her at home. Say something like this: "I've thought about it and girls who get to go to the mall alone with their friends are girls who need to show their parents consistently that they can be patient, helpful, and positive at home." You can fill in the blank here with whatever behaviors you are trying to instill. And just like that, their desire becomes leverage for their next step in growth.

Right about now, you might be thinking, "Renee, you are nuts. I *never* want her to go to the mall with her friends. I want to say no, no matter what." And I'll reply, "But remember the goal is that one day she won't live with you. No matter how hard that is to swallow, it is the truth of this parenting game."

They will need to leave us one day and so it is our job to make sure they can do these things without us. So work on the adult skills she will need at home for a bit. Catch her making mature choices. You can make home life the practice zone and the work on these skills can last as long as you need until you see she might be ready. As you see her getting closer to expected behaviors, you can begin to scaffold or support her along by going to the mall more often with her, demonstrating how we behave there, and by dropping her and her friends off at one end of the mall and heading in a different direction, nearby but not hovering over. In this new approach, you have an opportunity to connect and correct at the same time. You connect by hearing your child and correct by using it to leverage the mature behavior you've been looking for. We don't get these chances very often, so take it!

ACTION STEP: Envision yourself saying yes to something you've said no to in the past. How could you use this as an opportunity to help them grow? How could you give this to them in parts or with scaffolds as they learn their way through it?

THE WHOLE CHILD IN BLOOM

Your child is so much more than their behaviors!

In my husband's closet he has a retro sign that used to hang in his Grandma Evy's laundry room. It is a "Recipe for a Happy Day," simple advice that could help you change your day. While reading it one day, it dawned on me—the **Recipe for Helping Your Children Grow and Bloom:**

1. Sprinkle seeds of love (a love that lasts, no matter what).
2. Ground them with roots of understanding (that allows each child to have their unique strengths, interests, and needs met).
3. Provide warmth (that surrounds the child in comfort and trust).
4. Provide water and safety (that cleanses the dirt and harm away).
5. Let the growth begin.
6. Each flower will take on their own stem and their pace of growth will be unique to them.
7. Provide them with care and experiences that lead to physical, cognitive, social, emotional, and linguistic growth.
8. Factor in all the people and experiences which surround and support the child.
9. Suddenly, you will see the whole child bloom.

This kind of cultivating in kids means realizing that they are first and foremost a whole person, made up of much more than their singular behaviors. It is through recognizing this that we see that we don't simply sprinkle seeds and expect them to grow, just like we don't simply tell a child to be nice or stop fighting with their siblings and hope it happens. We pick the perfect patch of sun or preplan the environment so that it supports the positive growth.

We engage their whole self into that environment by narrowing in on all the things that enrich and motivate the child and make sure to include those things in their life. What helps them calm down? What is their leverage? Where are they in their growth and development? What are their talents, both hidden and obvious? What do they need to succeed and show us everything they've got?

As part of this we also recognize the behaviors that are creeping up (the weeds) and we work to identify them. We teach, model, and practice replacement behaviors for them, praise the new behaviors, and replace them with fun and function. They are so much more than these behaviors even if the weeds (or behaviors) seem loud, bold, bothersome, or obnoxious. So we do our best to notice the good stuff, the big blooms that *are* happening, even if they are happening at God's rate, not ours. Recognize what doesn't fit the child's life and pull those things out so that we can replace them with what works.

ACTION STEP: Draw a circle for each of your children. Fill that circle with ten lines. Write everything that anyone should know about them if they were to understand the whole child. Include strengths, needs, interests, leverage, calm down preferences, academics, social skills, family life, spiritual connection, and talents. This is called The Big Ten of Seeing the Whole Child. Do not include their specific negative behavior in this list. Keep those behaviors in mind for the next step and place them as dots on the edge of the circle. This symbolizes to you, or to anyone you are describing them to, that your child's behaviors are not part of them, but instead just one way they might interact or bump up against the world.

STOP BEHAVIORS

The whole child bumps up against the world.
You can love the child and not their behavior.

When connecting to your child and getting to know their whole person, it is important to recognize the ins and outs of how they bump up against the world. We could just focus on how wonderful they are and avoid the tough conversations and contemplation around their sticking points, places where the behavior they exhibit is getting in the way of their life's fun and function.

Those points you added to the outside edges of their Whole Child Circle are where they get themselves in trouble, and we really don't want the focus to be on trouble. We'd rather it be on teaching and learning so that they *can* have fun and function. So we use The Big Ten of Seeing the Whole Child to know what they need and like and *can* do to help us teach, model, and practice around what they need help with.

Most parents zero in first on these behaviors. This is because behaviors are loud, obnoxious, bothersome, and are often against the social rules. Parents want those behaviors to go away so they put most of their energy into addressing these behaviors, saying "*Stop* it" and "*Quit* it!" I want to suggest to you something I think you already know—telling kids to stop behaviors doesn't work. In fact, for whatever reason, it often makes the behavior get worse or continue day after day. **So put an end to the stop its!**

Instead, make a list of these behaviors when you see them. And think to yourself, what category are these behaviors falling into? I have found in my practice and studies that there are three main categories for negative behaviors: hurting, fussing, and disrespect. There are three other categories where behaviors show up that take away from a child's fun and function, and those are behaviors that show up in these situations: learning time, social time, and life skill time.

You've probably heard that awareness is the first step. So it's time to shine a light or some awareness on the exact Stop Behaviors you wish would go bye-bye. What are those behaviors from your child that are driving you crazy and fooling with the child's function and fun? You cannot begin to change behaviors coming from your child if you first haven't named them.

I will give you a quick example. I was visiting with a family. They thought I was there to help them with their child's never-ending pottying issues. Little did they know that the pottying issues played second fiddle to the disrespect of the child not listening and looking when Mom and Dad were talking. They hadn't seen with their own eyes that their child completely ignored their words. They thought it was just about the potty training. My job was to help them see it started with the listening. We had to name this first thing as first and evident so that we could change that behavior as a first step to fixing the potty training.

ACTION STEP: We will talk in more detail about the different types of behaviors, but for now, consider this: What are your child's sticking points, the behaviors standing in the way of fun and function? You know what these are in your gut. You've seen them in action and I want to give you permission to make those behaviors go away. Remember you can love the child and not their behavior. The two are not one and the same. It's just behavior, and not your child, that you want to go bye-bye.

VERBS, NOT ADJECTIVES

Behaviors are verbs, not overarching adjectives.

When presenting to a group of parents, I usually begin the session by asking for parents to call out behaviors that they would like to go bye-bye. These parents came to this session for a reason, so the hands go up right away and the answers usually fall into one of the first three categories I mentioned—hurting, fussing, or disrespect. I hear hurting behaviors like kicking, biting, shoving, and calling names. I hear fussing behaviors like whining, crying, screaming, and begging. And I hear disrespectful behaviors like eye rolling, walking away, not listening, and smart-mouthing. All of these behaviors qualify as behaviors because they are verbs or actions that a person takes. Notice they are not characteristics or descriptions of the child's personality.

When I isolate behaviors into categories, it helps me to see them as just behaviors and not part of the person. I can literally pick that behavior up and plop it into a category. Usually I do this right on a white board or poster at the session. This helps the parents see that these behaviors can be pulled away from the child and are not weaved into their soul. **They are just a thing sitting between the child and another person or their world.**

Within every session I also inevitably get a few descriptors as examples of a child's behavior. A parent might raise their hand and say, "My child is rude or jealous." And here is where I have to step in and help them qualify what they are trying to say about their child's behavior. Rude to me might be different than rude to them. So saying that a child is rude is not a behavior, it is an adjective and a subjective adjective at that. Listing a verb behavior makes the identification of behavior much more objective. So I ask them to narrow it down to a verb.

- What does rude look like?
- What action equals rude?
- Give me a verb that describes what the child does that is rude.

I might hear a few verbs in their description, so I ask them to narrow down again to the most common or most demanding behavior. I might hear them say, "He interrupts all the time." *Ahhhh!* I see this now. Now I can picture what it might look like. I will need more info to clarify the scene so I ask questions:

- What does it look like?
- Who does it happen with?
- Where are they when it happens?
- What happens right before it?
- What happens right after it?
- When does it happen?
- How often is it happening?

Connecting to exactly what the behavior is helps me to connect to next steps for that behavior. It is essential to pause and identify the behaviors and the details around it to make those behaviors go away. We've connected to the full child now. The good, the helpful, and the things that are standing in the way of fun and function. Now it's time to connect to our parenting.

ACTION STEP: Make a list of Stop Behaviors and categorize them (hurting, fussing, or disrespectful) and then ask yourself the above questions to help you narrow down further.

Part Three

Parenting Styles

EGGSHELLS AND POWERPLAYS

Identifying your parenting style will help you better understand your communication and connection with your children.

The next step in this process is to pause into our parenting styles and see where we fall. You've heard all the different scientific terms of parenting styles: authoritarian, authoritative, etc. I don't know about you, but it is difficult for me to keep it all straight. I don't think we have time to waste on the intricacies of these two terms or any other in the world of parenting. We need to get down to business and decide where we fall on the spectrum of parenting. We need to ask ourselves how we can most effectively use our style and what we know about children and behavior to inform our next steps.

Speaking of next steps, do your kids feel like they are walking on eggshells around you? Do they feel like you're the boss and it's not worth it to mess with you? Being the boss and being bossy are two different things and I think it's important to tease that out.

First, being the boss means being the author of the rules, an essential responsibility of being the adult in the room. Being bossy means *correct, correct, correct,* while forgetting connection. Bossy Parents in my book (literally) mean those that have forgotten connection (everything we read in section one) and they focus on their expectations, spending most of their time telling others what to do. So the Bossy Parent is on one end of the parenting spectrum.

Then of course we have the other end of the spectrum—the Polite Parent who is usually walking on eggshells around their child. Some might say being polite equates to being gentle and not firm, and I would agree. I think it starts out being gentle and flexible and suddenly you are the Polite Parent. Making suggestions, kindly asking for requests, and letting the child rule the roost all to ensure the child doesn't feel like you are the boss.

The problem is, you are the boss, right? Because if you are not, I guess the other person in the room is the boss—and who wants a three year old or a thirteen year old to be the boss of their house? That's scary for everyone, including the three year old and the teenager. If you are the parent in the room, that means you are the adult in the room, and that means you have to be the boss. **We need an author of the rules in the home and whether you like it or not, that means you have to have the final say.** This means you have to be the "because I said so" parent.

But, and this is a big *but,* it doesn't have to be bossy. It just has to be clear and it has to be connected. Your parenting also cannot be too polite because polite parenting means you become busy making suggestions instead of identifying the clear-cut expectations. When expectations are clear, everyone feels safer and in the end, we have less behaviors.

1. Connect four times more than correct (you do this connection because you love your child) so that you can correct when you need to.
2. Make your connection less polite and more genuine moments that show you are present and care about their day.
3. Author the rules and do it clearly without being too bossy.

ACTION STEP: Do your kids feel like they are walking on eggshells around you or are you walking on eggshells around them? Understanding this will help you figure out the power differential in your home. What if there were no eggshells, just clear-cut rules authored by you and connection that was genuine and sincere?

RESOURCE: A great book that highlights why parents need to be the author of the rules is *The Soul of Discipline* by Kim John Payne.

DISCIPLINE DOESN'T HAVE TO BE A FOUR-LETTER WORD

To discipline is to teach, but some people think of discipline as a four-letter word that has no place in a loving home. They are wrong. You are your child's first teacher, so give your parenting a dose of discipline.

Discipline doesn't have to be a dirty word in your home. In fact, when you think about it, there are several positive four-letter words associated with discipline.

1. NEED— Children don't know they need discipline, and they may not act like they enjoy your boundaries, especially when you are in the heat of a battle. But the right kind of discipline involving structure, routines, and expectations gives a child a clear path to follow. How can a child begin to do what is expected in his home if the guidelines of his family life are fuzzy? How can a child know his responsibilities around the home unless these jobs and roles have been thoroughly explained to him? How can a child know not to make bad choices if he doesn't know the clear implications of the choices? Children **need** discipline to understand their world and their place within it.

2. SAFE— When children know what their days will bring, they feel **safe**. They know they can count on Mom or Dad to follow through on what they say (good or bad), and that makes them feel secure. Sure, the negative consequences of making a bad choice can make a child feel like they are suffering, but this kind of suffering helps to instill a boundary on what they can and cannot do. They feel **safe** in knowing that every time they make a specific choice, an identified consequence will follow. There will be no room for question, no room for worry, and only a clear understanding of expectations and boundaries. Their little world will feel predictable and **safe.**

3. LOVE— Yes, you can **love** your child and at the same time put boundaries on their behavior. When you shape your parenting with structure, you are giving your child what they **need** to be **safe.** Giving them these two gifts will make them feel **loved.** It is not a **love** that is conditional on behavior but one that is rooted in understanding what is best for them. This kind of **love** does not change. It stays the same and so does the behavior expectation. They can trust it and feeling safe in these expectations makes them feel loved. You can help ensure that they know they are **loved** no matter what by letting them know that you **love** them even when you don't love their choices.

ACTION STEP: So now that we see that discipline is an essential part of any good parenting practice, think about where you can add structure and secure boundaries to your child's life. Do you have a plan for how your children should act at the dinner table? Does your child know the list of rules for behavior when friends come to visit? Have you clearly stated the general guidelines for being polite, responsible, and caring individuals? When you go to a new place do you set up "on the spot" boundaries for behavior?

ASSUME NOTHING, EXCUSE NOTHING. TEACH, MODEL, AND PRACTICE EVERYTHING

Welcome to the world of teaching, where you will be your child's most important teacher.

Assume Nothing: Whether they are "threenagers" or teenagers, it's likely that your kid might act like they know everything. But the truth is, they know nothing—unless they've had some teaching to fill the gaps of what they don't understand. With all the newness that each transition brings, we as their parents have to lean into our teaching role to help them grow and get through it.

They've never been five before, or maybe twelve is new for them. Wherever their spot within their growing years is, they are just getting to it. They have no idea what you know and you can't assume they know your expectations. Whether you'd like to admit it or not, they cannot read your mind. Even if you continually say, "You should know better!" they simply don't know.

So assume they know nothing and it is your job to teach, model, and practice everything. They need your help to decode the rules and expectations and learn how to function within your family. They won't figure these things out by osmosis or through incidental learning alone, they need explicit instruction right from their parent.

Excuse Nothing: Parents call me and they tell me about their child's outbursts and out of control behavior. They called because they know in their gut it's just not okay, but they absolutely hate to pin down that behavior as a negative thing about their child, so they coat it with excuses.

"Well, he just beats up his brother because he's very bright and likes to be in control. The little brother gets in his way, and you can imagine how frustrated he is, so he often just goes off on his baby brother. Boys will boys."

And I say, yes, boys will be boys and men will also be boys until we determine what behaviors don't fit the function of the family. We must extinguish these behaviors, along with the excuses that make them go on and on.

Here are some honest excuses I have heard throughout the years...

- "She's the only girl, so we just know it's best to make her happy. If she isn't happy, ain't nobody happy."
- "Well, he's our little spitfire. He gets mad and throws things. You know how the wild child is. Every family has one."
- "He's our little genius and I guess that's why he's just so rude to everyone. He simply has a hard time dealing with kids who can't compete with his intelligence level."
- "Well, girls will be girls. Moody, moody, moody!"
- "Boys will be boys, you know, knocking everything over."
- "Well, he is so amazing on the soccer field, we just hate to draw attention to the bad behavior so much. We think it helps him be more aggressive in his games."
- "Her grades are so good, and she puts so much pressure on herself to be perfect. We'd hate to call her out on her tone and make her think we think small things like how she speaks to us matter more than her great grades."

Enough! It's time to say enough!

The excuses make these behaviors go on and on. You must cut them off. You must name the behavior to claim it and change it.

Let's get real so our really bright kiddos can also be really kind (wouldn't that be a dream) and our first-born control freak can finally learn he doesn't always get his way (*ahhh* how much better would his days be if he learns this earlier rather than later).

Behavior choices—like hurting, fussing, and being disrespectful—must be addressed. We must nip these behaviors in the bud if we want our children to thrive. Making excuses for their actions may provide short-term relief for us as their parents, but their future bosses and spouses will thank us if we allow them to face natural consequences and next steps when their self-regulation is out of whack now.

We cannot excuse a child's impatience or aggression by attributing it to their brightness or athleticism. It's crucial to prioritize good behavior as the most important skill they can develop, as it will serve them in every area of their lives. Imagine a world filled with compassionate and kind geniuses and humble and generous sports heroes. Imagine a future where your child learns that to be a friend or spouse means to sacrifice something for the betterment of the whole. These are the lessons that family life can give your child. Parents who use excuses end up taking away the chance to change these behaviors for the betterment of their child.

Teach, Model, and Practice Everything: Here's where you come in. Assume your child is a blank slate, a little sponge waiting to soak up the good stuff. Teach them how to share, how to calm down when they're feeling out of control, and yes, even how to eat their carrots so they don't hurt Grandma's feelings at the Thanksgiving table.

And guess what? They won't learn these skills in a classroom or on the soccer field as well as they would learn them from you and your approaches to teaching what matters most. Your teaching time is like gold. It happens outside of the moment, it should involve modeling and exemplifying what the expectations are in this home.

Then you set them out to practice and coach them along through their day-to-day interactions, pausing to reteach and rewinding when things just don't fit the norm.

You are a teacher whether you wanted to be or not.

Consider your structure. Do you have a system for how and when and where you teach these things? Do you have a list of things that you know you need to teach?

Think about your tone and keep it steady, not too harsh but clear enough that they know it's important. Add in connection and humor and ways to remember what you've taught them so it sticks. Whether it be a new mantra, a key phrase, or a witty one liner that reminds them to get it together. Whatever you do, make your teaching a balance between connection and correction. Then when you see the good outweigh the bad, praise it.

The only assumption you can make is that they likely don't know how else to respond. The only excuse is their parent has taught them how to behave or shown them that their actions affect others negatively. It's time to move past assumptions and excuses and focus on teaching.

ACTION POINT: Now, let's do a little self-reflection. What excuses have you been using to dodge the tough conversations about your kid's behavior? "Oh, he's just having a rough day!" Sound familiar? Time to pull those excuses out of your back pocket and toss them in the trash. Building awareness of these excuses is the first step toward addressing the behaviors that hinder their social and emotional development. Assume they don't know how to do it, and it's time to tackle those behaviors head-on. By embracing the mantra of "Assume Nothing, Excuse Nothing. Teach, Model, and Practice Everything," you'll be well on your way to raising respectful, kind, and capable future citizens.

GO LIGHT ON POLITE

Chop off the "Okay?" "Please?" and "Alright?" and see if your child finds your requests more clear and doable.

Every parent dreams of having polite children who mind their manners and say their pleases and thank yous without having to be told. It seems perfectly logical that modeling politeness to your children will evoke the same polite responses back from them. This is why it is natural for thoughtful parents to make a heartfelt effort to model politeness for their kids. There is nothing wrong with this and I do believe that the modeling of politeness is essential to helping kids learn how to act towards others.

But, and this is a big *but,* it is essential that we don't let politeness take over the need for correction. In the name of politeness a parent might make requests that are coated in these questions or tack on requests: Please? Okay? Alright?

Here's how it might sound:

- "It's time to get your coat on, okay?"

or maybe parents will say,

- "Please be nice to your brother, okay?" (a double tack on)

or they might say,

- "It's time to go to bed, alright?"

You might be thinking, why wouldn't I tack on a "Please?" or "Okay?" at the end? Isn't that the perfect way to model how to ask for something? The problem isn't in tacking it on and modeling how to ask nicely, the problem is that when you make these requests, it's usually not a request but a command or a necessary next step they need to take. So there is no room in the request for a suggestion or yes or no question. Yes or no questions and suggestions show up when we say those tack on words: "Please?" "Okay?" and "Alright?"

You can imagine what the next word out of your child's mouth will be if you ask them or request that they do something and then put an "Okay?" at the end of the sentence. Their answer very likely could be "NO!" So then the parent just set themselves up for that "NO!" Don't set yourself up. Instead, be clear and not so polite. Just tell them what the next step is without asking if they would like to or if they could please.

Here is a clear-cut example:

- "Time for bed. Choose your pajamas. Up, up, up, you go! To the top of the bed."

If we add in the suggestion words it might look like:

- "Time for bed, okay? Please choose your pajamas, alright? Can you please get into your bed?"

With these phrases we lose before we even begin. Skip them and you will skip a world of headaches.

Avoiding politeness doesn't mean you will be rude, but you will be more clear, without any confusion about what exactly the child needs to do.

ACTION STEP: Listen to your requests that you make of your children. Are you sugarcoating them with "Please?" "Alright?" and "Okay?" How's that going for you? Are they listening or looking the other way and not accomplishing what you are asking them to do? Chop off the "Okay?" "Please?" and "Alright?" and see if your child finds your requests more clear and doable.

PARENTING FLIP-FLOPS

Flip-flopping your style wears you out and confuses the kids.

When I meet with a family to help support their parenting, I usually ask the mom and the dad or whomever are the key caregivers to meet with me together first. I want to get to know them together and see how they counteract each other's style of parenting and see where they might lean too much towards polite or land in the correction zone without being clear and kind and connected.

Usually Mom and Dad are parenting from different angles or perspectives, where one of them is the corrector and one of them is the connector. It is rare to find them on the same page when they call me, so the first step is to help them find a common ground. Beyond flip-flopping between their two styles, parents also flip-flop on their own.

Mom might start off sweet and polite when trying to get her kids to do their homework. She doesn't want to ruin their day, she excuses them on their missing work, remembering they are just kids and thinking to herself, "I need to give them grace." *And then,* they don't listen over and over again and suddenly she is screaming at the top of her lungs. The kids are confused by this extreme change in her approach, but it happens time and time again with families. Trying to be polite only lasts so long and then we end up losing our minds.

So skip the polite upfront and go with a good middle of the line, clear-cut, matter-of-fact but kind approach. This will help you stay steady and avoid the high-low extremes. Then when you want to connect and talk softly to your kids, give them extra special treatment, or if you need to get serious about something dangerous or an inexcusable behavior, you can bump up a little more naturally to a serious tone or bend down to the soft and loving tone. **Staying in the middle makes the flipping and flopping less extreme and helps everyone feel safe, okay, and that they can handle this.**

If you cannot find the middle ground in your parenting tone and approach, stick with one or the other. Be polite and own it as it is. Staying steady with your politeness will help your kids know what to expect even if they eventually might overtake you. Or be bossy and keep it that way. The kids will come to recognize you at that level and it will honestly help because kids just need consistency.

ACTION STEP: How are you and your parenting partner flipping and flopping? Do you each parent in extremely different ways, so the kids don't know what to expect? Do you yourself flip-flop from kind and sweet to bullying and brash? Discuss how your flip-flopping might be confusing the scenario. How could you round out the flipping and flopping and replace it with more consistency with your tone, rules, procedures, and outcomes?

BIBLE VERSE: "I wish you were either one or the other!" (Revelations 3:15).

YOUR CHILD'S BIGGEST INFLUENCER

Be intentional about who and what is influencing your child.

There are so many entities out there that would love to be your child's influencer: Netflix, Girl Scouts, sports heroes, rock stars, their teachers, their peers, Youtuber sensations... but what about you?

Think about the time spent in your home and who or what is having the most influence on your child. How could you increase your influence on your child? This doesn't have to mean that you spend more time with them, although I do think that your time with them is always time well spent.

Of course kids want to branch out beyond Mom and Dad, but how can you influence what they consume and what influences them? I will walk through my husband Toby and my approach based on what we wanted to be the most influential parts of our child's life.

1. **FAMILY:** Our inner circle (siblings, Mom, and Dad). We really felt like what happens in our home will directly mirror how they act when they leave our home. We spent the time it took to refine and support positive sibling and parent relationships, which involved respect and dignity for each other's differences, needs, and a common ground where we enjoyed each other's company. We did this through time together. Ironically, as I reflect on this, I see that these four things were the exact ways my own parents influenced my siblings and me. The circle and cycle of influence continues. I guess I was so influenced by my parents that I took these things with me.

- **Meals at the table.**
  These are preempted by grace. We still do this at every meal when everyone is home.

- **Prayer pause before the first person heads to bed.**
  We still do this as a way to stop and thank the Lord for the day, pray for those we know who are in need of support, and look ahead to our worries of tomorrow. This moment to lean on a higher power was on purpose to help them see they need God to help them day-to-day.

- **Regular getaways at special places we now call our own.**
  We found special spots that we dreamed of getting away to and despite finances being challenged at times, we always made this a priority. This created lasting memories and moments that influenced the formation of our family.

- **Extended family connections and stories of who came before them.**
  It was so important to our children's formation to know the stories of our grandparents—the lives, accomplishments, and personalities of their own grandparents. It was important for my children to connect to people like cousins, aunts, and uncles who shared their history and their gene pool. Our family members are the kind of influencers I want our kids to have.

2. **FRIENDS:** Toby and I were one of the first couples to get married in both of our friend groups, so if you watched our wedding from a bird's eye view, you would have seen a ton of laughter and twentysomethings from across our high school, college, and young adult lives partying it up together. I remember that the night of our rehearsal dinner, Toby's good friend Rob described him as the most loyal friend. We both value our long-standing friends and those twentysomething kids are now in mid-life after raising their own twentysomethings! Our kids know their kids, we make a point to connect through visits and special occasions like graduations and baptisms (we are each

other's kids' godparents). They've been there for us through our losses. Our kids have witnessed these friendships and this has helped encourage them to place value on these kind of connections as they foster their own lifelong people. These friends of ours have become like aunts and uncles to our kids. In fact, just today Toby said he was in a text chain between his buddy Matt and our twenty-one-year-old son discussing some upcoming concert they all want to attend together. Matt and the many friends we each have are the kind of influencers I want our kids to have!

3. **EDUCATION:** As an educator and someone who was blessed to attend superior public and private schools and a university that encouraged me to be a critical thinker, I value that our kids get the chance to be influenced by the greats. The greatest stories through history, the greatest characters and the lessons they learned through their trials, the greatest new ways to see the same old experience, and the greatest teachers who have told them beyond what we have already told them—that they can do what they set their mind to, that they have been gifted with a unique set of skills and talents that should not go to waste. So we have purposefully put ourselves into situations where we could help connect them to a schooling experience that could change their trajectory. When our daughter needed a change of schools and settings, we listened to the call, even if the price point was beyond what was in our wallet. We have found that around every corner we've found a way to give them a chance at an education to influence them. We survived the big tax bill when they went to public schools, weeded through the Catholic high school expenses and although we are still working like crazy to pay those college bills, we don't regret for a single moment that we invested in the influence a good education can give our children.

4. **WORK and SERVICE:** Toby and I both are blessed to say we love our work and the calling within it that allows us to show our kids that putting passion into what you do can be a way

to reflect God's love. We shared stories about the work we do with them while sitting at the dinner table, talking through how to solve problems and make things better day-to-day. We also wanted them to see that they were called in some way to work in service to support our community. From an early age, we found opportunities to put our good skills to work to serve, so we created a breakfast service once a month with friends from our community at a local community service center. Our kids helped to make the breakfast, pour the orange juice, set the tables, and they learned that their world was bigger than our home. They recognized the community members as their neighbors and like all good neighbors, you take care of each other. That means showing up and working together. Since then, our kids have found their own ways to work and serve that are different than what we started, but they are their own. I believe the experiences we gave them as children influenced the servant leaders and workers they've become.

5. **ART and NATURE:** Our kids could tell you that every summer we made a plan to take at least two field trips a month, if not one a week. These field trips were a way for me to help them experience things they may not have the chance to connect with in our home or at their school. An art museum or sculpture park, a nature trail or view from a hillside looking over the city, or a photography exhibit with history lessons embedded in it. Much to their dismay, these kinds of trips also showed up on their spring breaks and vacation getaways because I wanted them to see beyond the beach. We also tried to help them find their own connections to art by sharing our love for art with them until they found their own way. They laugh at my constant random craft of the season but I see that they seek opportunities to craft and create now too. They begged us for concert tickets to their favorite bands, so we gave in because we also trudged them along to our own favorite venues and concerts. A love of music, art, and nature has a world of influences that help kids broaden their perspectives.

6. **FAITH:** The faith connections in the above connections go without saying. Faith through our family and friend traditions. Faith through our leaning on others like old pals and wise elders to help us through hard times. Faith connections in our community and through their educational experiences, and faith connections through their love of music and the beautiful picture on the wall.

If you are truly present in their day-to-day life, they will most likely want to share with you, learn from you, and get your expert opinion and critique. And the experiences and people you place into their life will become the lasting influence that moves with them to the next generation. They will learn to be kind by watching you and seeing what you value.

Be careful if a specific artist or influencer is the new voice they listen to over you. If you don't like what they are experiencing, don't be afraid to curb the connection, but make sure to fill the space with something else that's grounded in what you wish for them.

Giving them a balance and depth of influence early on and throughout their growing years can help to influence how they see and interact in the world. You don't have to do this through lecturing them, instead it can come naturally through the kind of focused influences that are just weaved into their life.

ACTION STEP: Take a moment to look through the above six influence categories. Determine if you have some gaps that are being filled by outside influences that you aren't too sure about. If so, fill those gaps with the kind of influences, experiences, and people you want your child to connect to. Be intentional about who and what are influencing your child.

PARENTING BLISS PART ONE

Make sure it's "because I said so" without losing the love.

There are two types of parenting: "because I said so" (BISS) parenting and "because you said so" (BYSS) parenting. We previously discussed the intricate details of what it means to be a Bossy or Polite Parent. I know you are waiting for that middle line of parenting and now it's time to bring in a glimmer of hope. There is a middle line—Parenting BLISS.

Notice my acronym BLISS still has the BISS. That's because the rules of the universe insist that parents must be in charge. You are the author of the rules because you have to be. It's way too scary to allow a child to be the author of the rules. So lean into BISS without going all the way there. This means you will need to begin to parent with a bottom-line approach that involves the "because I said so" phrasing (at times). Granted, there are times for children to be heard and yes, if you want any semblance of power, you must give them power through giving them a voice. But in the end, no matter what, all decisions have to run through you—the adult, the authority. There is no room at the bottom-line for "because you said so." Saying "because I said so" all the time will get you in trouble and make you hypercorrective. We need you to balance that correction with connection, so I added in the "L."

The "L" is for the love and like of your child. Both Bossy and Polite Parents are doing what they are doing with *love* as their mainstream. The Bossy Parent feels like if they love their child, they will put boundaries all over them, and if their child loves them back, they will obey. The Polite Parent feels like if they love their child, they would never, ever let them suffer through crying or missing out on what they want. They would whittle away at anything that might make a child sad and weed it out of their life, all in the name of loving the child. I am not saying that these parents love their children too much or not enough. There really is no way you could love your children too much, and simply put you can't help but love your kids. It's ingrained in you. You love them and they love you. There's no arguing about this, no questioning the love of any parent, it's just that some parents get confused as to what love is.

When our own kids were little, I used to say to them, "I could never stop loving you," and then they would give me scenarios to see if they might stump me and my undying love.

Peter said to me one time, "What if I robbed a bank mom?"

"I'd still love you."

Mick tried, "What if I told the biggest lie ever?"

"I'd still love you."

Evy blurted out, "What if I called someone a bad word, Mom?"

"I'd still love you."

If they did drugs, if they failed out of school, if they cheated on a final exam, if they crashed our new car, I would still love them. You see, I simply can't stop loving my children and you can't stop loving your kids either. However, **the big eye opener is that it is possible to love your child and despise their behavior**. Look, I can't stand stealing, lying, cussing, drugs, failing, cheating, or reckless driving. I can name these things as things I despise and cut them off from the person who does them. **These things are behaviors, they are not people.** Love the sinner, not the sin.

In fact, if you find that there are behaviors that you want to see go away, you must first come to despise them, so that you can begin to name them. Then and only then will you be able to stop them. Stopping them doesn't mean you are squelching your child's self-esteem. It does mean you love them and they love you, and you love them enough to help the behavior that has wedged itself between you go away. It's the behavior that is wrecking your homelife that has to go bye-bye, not the child. This makes everything way less emotional because it is less personal. Now we can begin to implement the rest of the approaches necessary to achieve parenting BLISS.

ACTION STEP: Make a point to specifically reinforce to your children that your love resembles the unconditional love of God. . . no matter what!

BIBLE VERSE: "No, in all these things we are more than conquerors through him who loved us. For I am sure that neither death nor life, nor angels nor rulers, nor things present nor things to come, nor powers, nor height nor depth, nor anything else in all creation, will be able to separate us from the love of God in Christ Jesus our Lord" (Romans 8:37-39).

Part Four

Parenting Bliss

BEGINNING THE BLISS: DON'T BE SUCH A SUCKER

It's okay to let kids suffer.

Suffering In Order to Grow in Civil Skills

Okay let's face it, life is not a bowl of cherries without any pits. There will be ups and downs and your child will actually be growing as they deal with the downs. They will learn how it feels to be disappointed, and they will get better and better at getting through the disappointments when they get chances to suffer through them. So BLISSful parents do not go along "safety netting" their kids all day, every day. They allow the children to suffer and survive through their choices even if that means losing out or lots of tears. They recognize their child is in motion and these little bumps will build their character. Here's an example to help you see how our culture has shifted towards children being raised without suffering:

Don't Be Such A Sucker

What child doesn't love a trip to the bank? It's one of the errands on Mom's list of places to go that kids simply don't mind attending. Why is this? SUCKERS!

I was in the drive-through line at our bank, back in 2012. It was one of the final days of summer, so I had a carful of kids. There were big kids and little kids. Kids that were mine and kids that were other people's kids. Everyone knew what their prize would be if they stayed quiet while I tried to hear the teller's directions over the speaker.

The teller asked, "Do you have children in the car and are they allowed to have a sucker?" These were her typical questions. She was so kind to ask them, and I responded, "I have four children in the car, and yes, they are allowed to have a sucker. Thank you so much."

However, the teller went beyond her call of duty with her next question. With one quick question she opened up a can of worms instead of that yummy jar of suckers. She said, "And what flavors do they want?"

My children's eyes lit up because not only did they get a sucker, but they got to choose the flavor! Holy Moly! Life is good!

What I want to know is when did things change? When did we move from offering a special treat, to appeasing our children's every want and desire? This shift, I fear, is what is creating havoc in many of our homes. This question of **"What do you want?"** changes the road ahead in our families as it puts the child in the driver's seat. I think the question stems from our need to avoid having our children suffer.

Maybe parents are thinking these things:

- "My children have a mind of their own, why would I want them to have to suffer through having a sucker they don't like?"
- "Wouldn't it be tortuous to expect them to sit quietly while I speak to the teller, and then give them a black raspberry sucker when they really wanted a watermelon one?"
- "What a horrible mother I would be if I didn't give them what they wanted! Shouldn't I give them what they want and deserve?"

Well, I guess *that* is the million-dollar question.

What do our children deserve?

Do children deserve special treats, or are special treats an added bonus to their expected behavior? This may sound radical, but I say children don't deserve anything for making good choices while you wait at the bank or when they act as they are expected to act.

Now, if the teller is nice enough to offer you a sucker, then you may have one, but the deal is: You get what you get and you don't have a fit. If you don't like the flavor you have received, then you kindly pass it on to your brother and ask if he would like to swap flavors. If no one wants to swap, you keep the sucker to share with your poor mother who has driven you all over town, or you simply throw it away when you get home. Is this logical or am I crazy?

Crazy is dooming our children to a life filled with constant pleasure and no suffering. This is because eventually life will deal them a "yucky sucker," and they won't know how to suffer gracefully because they've never had to do this before.

Back to our bank story: I kindly responded, "We are okay with whatever flavor we get," as my children cringed and groaned at me in the back seats. Then the teller said, "Thank you for being so easygoing. I just had a mom drive back through the line because the sucker I gave her wasn't her child's favorite, and she didn't want to hear him cry about it all the way home."

YIKES! Are you kidding me? Is this what we've resorted to?

Are these the life rules for children?

1. Get a treat for doing nothing out of the ordinary.
2. Cry as hard as you can when you don't like the treat.
3. Then your mother will beg for another free treat so that she doesn't have to listen to you suffer.

When it comes to freebies like suckers at the bank, there is no fussing. You get what you get and you don't have a fit. If children are allowed to throw a fit and get what they want, their parents are supporting negative behaviors.

If you do throw a fit, then you will get nothing. Mom or Dad *will not* contrive the perfect scenario to make your wishes come true. They *will not* coddle you until you calm down over your "horrible experience." Although this will be a challenge for parents, they will simply say, "Let me know when you are ready to join us or if you change your mind about your treat."

Then Mom and Dad will tune you out and not react to your fit so that you learn to regulate your emotions on your own.

Ahhhh isn't life with children so sweet?

ACTION STEP: I know many parents who would simply skip the bank. It's just too much for the parent to suffer through this suffering. They would sooner hire a babysitter to stay with the kids than have to push through a suffering moment where the child doesn't get the sucker they want. Don't skip the bank, in fact, take them to places where they will have to suffer through waiting and not getting what they want. Bring your children to these places as much as you can so that the child learns how to survive and make it through these moments. Protecting them through these situations might be a short-term solution, but the long-term outcome is a grown child who still throws temper tantrums or has mental breakdowns when things don't fit their ideals.

TEACH OUTSIDE THE MOMENT

No one can learn when they are on fire.

As we discussed before, parents often try to correct misbehavior in the heat of the moment, saying things like, "Stop it!" or "Quit it!" This is ineffective. Telling a child to stop misbehaving when they are upset is like telling someone on fire to simply stop burning. Instead, we should teach them the desired Go Behavior we want them to show us in these situations.

This new behavior won't come out of nowhere—we can't assume they know what to do differently, so trying to get them to turn their behavior around while they are on fire is also ineffective. It's very likely they don't know what to do or have the capacity to do it when they are steaming in the moment. That's where teaching comes in, but that teaching has to take place once they have calmed down. This can happen when they want to connect later or even the next day when you can anticipate a similar situation arising.

When I encourage parents to teach, I always mean, "Teach outside of the moment." Teaching in the heat of the moment simply won't work.

So pause, take a breath, and save your teaching for a time when your child is calm and you are calm. Wait for them to be receptive and motivated to learn a new way. If they're in the middle of an emotional struggle, they won't be able to learn and internalize the new skills you're trying to teach them, so don't waste your energy and time on teaching. Instead, make a note to yourself and think "Later, I need to teach." For now, just keep everyone safe, quiet the fire, and restore peace.

ACTION STEP: Consider starting a teaching journal. This journal can help you identify areas where your child might need additional guidance. To help organize your thoughts, try using a T-chart with "Teachable Moments" on one side and "Positive Moments" on the other. In the "Teachable Moments" column, jot down any situations or behaviors that you feel your child could learn from. During calm moments of connection, use these notes as a starting point for teaching.

THE TROUBLE TRAP

Trouble catching can take up all the air in the room. Release it to give space for flex and change.

When addressing misbehavior, it's easy to fall into a pattern of punishment. However, this often overlooks the opportunity for growth that "trouble situations" can bring a child. Instead of viewing your child as a "troublemaker" and yourself as the "trouble catcher," begin to see these moments as a chance to:

- Catch them being good.
- See small moments of growth and progress.
- Teach them new ways to respond.
- Model how it can look.
- Practice these new behavior responses.

You may not be actually saying, "You are in trouble" with your words, but your body language, facial expressions, or phrasing might give this impression.

Instead, go with the opposite upfront. When you walk into the behavior scene, clarify your own resolve and peace by saying the opposite, "You are not in trouble." This will signal to you to calm down and teach and signal to them that they can calm down and receive something from this.

To be real, I know you probably want to get them in trouble. I know inside you are steaming mad, you are probably thinking, "It's high time they learn," and "I will show them not to mess with me." These feelings are all justified because you are spent and done with their misbehavior.

But the truth is, if you throw them in "trouble" or throw out the words, "You are in trouble" you could quite possibly lose them. **"Trouble" changes everything.** If you or they lose your calm, you both lose the connection.

You say, "You are in trouble" and their body and mind tell them "Fight, Flight, Fawn, Freeze, or Fib." Trouble is traumatic. They have been there before and they don't want to go back there again, so they will do what it takes to protect themselves from trouble.

Trouble puts them in a corner and when people feel trapped, they often get themselves into second layers of trouble, such as:

- **Fighting** with words or physically.
- **Fleeing,** running, or escaping the scene.
- **Fawning,** doing whatever you say just to appease you even if they really did have a voice in the situation.
- **Freezing** up and saying or doing nothing so you feel like you are dealing with a brick wall.
- **Fibbing** to save face.

But when we simply reassure and say, "You are not in trouble," you release the trauma and you enter into trust. You humanize the situation where they messed up and help them to see they have a way out. **PAUSE, REWIND, ADJUST, RELEASE,** and **GROW.** They can begin to see themselves as dynamic and they can begin to use another F-word response:

- **Flex,** change, make it better, alter your stance, try again. It doesn't have to be this way.

This flex often takes time for kids. They will need space to do this so hovering over them while they pause or rewind or flex can create a second layer power struggle. Walk away, give them space, tell them to come to you when they have a flex plan. Giving them time and space to flex tells them "I think you are more than this."

Now of course as the author of the rules and keeper of time in your home, you have every right to go to "trouble" when the child isn't able to be dynamic and flex the situation. But even then, the trouble cannot last forever. The child needs to get back "on the horse" and try again tomorrow so you will have to open them up to trying again sometime soon, if you want this to be less about trouble and more about teaching and changing. The goal is to balance out all the trouble with teaching and turn it around.

In the end, make sure kids don't have to dwell too long in the shadow of their past mistakes. This allows them to dwell longer in the peace of knowing they have the space to mess up, flex, change, grow, and make their days more enjoyable as they do.

Through these moments you become stronger, not weaker, and your relationship and your child's growth will also become stronger.

ACTION STEP: You might feel a social pressure to allow your kids to be kids, or maybe you are feeling a natural pressure to show who's the author of the rules in your home and get your kids in trouble for the things they do that are out of line. I want to challenge you to find peace from those pressures in the middle zone that relies on teaching and supporting your child through their changes. Read Paul's letter to Colossians where he wrote to them to encourage them when they felt pressure and to help them find a deeper devotion to the Lord.

BIBLE VERSE: "Clothe yourselves with compassion, kindness, humility, meekness and patience. Bear with one another. . . and forgive one another" (Colossians 3:12).

KEEP IT SIMPLE

When it comes to talking to your kids, less is more. Less words and more pause can change the outcomes of your discussions.

We spend so much time talking to our kids. We've all been there. We feel like we are droning on like the teacher in the *Peanuts* cartoon or speaking to a brick wall.

Consider this. Have you spent time. . .

- **Lecturing** your kids about why bonking their brother over the head with a block is not a good idea?
- **Debating** with kids about whether 8:00 p.m. is too late for another snack?
- **Giving kids a spiel** on how to be polite at Grandma's house?
- **Completing a discourse** on why they need a summer job?
- **Barking commands** that go on and on?
- **Shouting directions** that are too detailed to be followed accurately?

The good news is you are not alone. Parents everywhere are talking in circles. The bad news is that all that talking means we are going nowhere fast and our big points are getting lost in the language. Odds are you lost them after the first three to five words.

So what is a parent to do? Keep it simple. Instead of outlining a two-hundred-word paragraph, simply say the first three words and then pause on purpose, then say the next three words, and pause and repeat until they are focused on what you are saying. Then everything you are saying is meaningful and necessary.

What happens when we talk in long lectures is that we go on and on and cloud the real point we are trying to make with too many extraneous words. So like Mom used to do in her flower garden, **prune away what is not necessary and get to the point.** You can do this by simply saying the first three words. Let's take the bonking your brother lecture for example:

The *long* lecture goes like this: "Jonny, I can't believe you just hit your brother over the head with a hard block. We can't do this, because it hurts way too much and your brother gets so sad and cries and you just keep playing along and that is not okay. I am not sure what your problem is and why you cannot get the point of this but you two just need to get along."

How can we say this without breaking the word bank?

Let's try three to five words at a time, with pauses:

Jonny *(the parent doesn't say a word and the long pause gets the child's attention).*
I just saw you hit. *(pause)*
Hitting hurts. *(pause)*
Hitting is not okay. *(pause)*
Sometimes brothers get mad, *(pause)*
but they do not hit. *(pause)*
Sometimes brothers take toys, *(pause)*
but they do not hit. *(pause)*
Sometimes brothers get sad, *(pause)*
but they do not hit. *(pause)*
When you are mad or sad, *(pause)*
you can say it with words *(pause)*
or you can walk away.

Remember to keep your dialogue simple, direct and clear.

This is especially true if you are in the heat of a power struggle, which I call the fire pit. If a child was truly in a fire pit and "on fire" with emotion or behavior, then we would need to pause and keep our words short and clear. Stop, drop, and roll. When kids are on fire, they can't process, so there is no need to spend time dousing them with language-filled lectures.

ACTION STEP: Next time you start your lecture, have your spouse or friend record it. Count the words before you pause. Begin to gain a consciousness around your word count and purposeful pausing. I pray you will find the Holy Spirit is in the breath, silence, and pause time. That connection to the Holy Spirit will breathe life and love into your words when you speak again.

LESS WORDS, MORE EXTRAS TO REPLACE THE WORDS

Subtracting the fluff words and descriptors means our kids will hear the essential information. It means we can carve out space for extras that can enhance our connections.

We already learned that when trying to get your kids to listen, your phrases should be key phrases that you use regularly. You should repeat them a few times in order to get their attention instead of going on and on in lecture format. Here are some of the key phrases that help lessen the lecture in our family life:

- Nice Gets Nice and *(pause)* Nasty Gets Nothing
- "Me First" *(pause)* Goes Last
- What Will You Choose to do—Stay, Play, or Walk Away?
- First _____ Then _____
- Boys Who _____ Are Boys Who Will Need to _____
- Show Me
- Sit With Me, *(pause)* Let's Talk
- Step One _____ Step Two _____ Step Three ____

I'd say no more than three to five words at a time with a purposeful pause is exactly what they need, and lecture is exactly what they do not need.

Here's a quick example of what not to do:

> "Tommy! What are you doing? Don't hit the doggie on the head. Be nice to the doggie and pat her on the head nicely, like this, or stay away from the doggie and go play with your toys."

If we really need to get our point across without a lot of words and emotion, then try to bring it down to a more direct approach like this:

> No hit the doggie
> Yes love the doggie
> Yes pat the doggie *(gesturing gentle patting)*
> No hit the doggie

Make sure to repeat the same phrase and actions every time that situation arises again. If you repeat the same phrase every time it happens, your quick key phrases will become *the standard,* and this is another reason why you need short phrasing so you can remember what you said last time.

Life is busy and overwhelming and language can get in the way of processing through the day. If you speak too much, you won't have as much time to pause and think about what exactly needs to be said step by step.

Your child also cannot process all that language. You will be able to pause and breathe and get yourself to a calmer state and your child will be more tuned into you if they feel safe with your clear and kind tone. When we fail to breathe, we get more upset and it comes across in our tone.

Here's a common example of what not to do:

> "After you eat your breakfast and put your clothes on, we are going to go to Grandma's house, but first, we will drive by Daddy's office and drop off something for Daddy. At Grandma's house, we are going to go swimming and have fun."

Try this approach instead and add simple images drawn on a scrap piece of paper for even better communication:

> "First, breakfast" (*with image #1 of breakfast foods*).
> "Second, get ready" (*with image #2 of kids getting ready*).
> "Third, drive to Daddy's office" (*with image #3 of car driving to Daddy's office*).

"Then, GRANDAMA's to go SWIMMING! Yeah! FUN, FUN, FUN!" (*with image #4 of Grandma's house*).

This may seem like a cold and simple-minded communication style, and you may worry that it won't help foster language skills in your child. I have found that the opposite is true. When a child can clearly hear you and clue in to what you are talking about, they can successfully maneuver through their day in more positive ways. In turn, this will open up more opportunity for positive language interactions with them as you read books, share stories with description, and help them describe their emotions. This is *not* how you will talk to them *all* day long. You will just use this style when it is important that they listen.

Here's one more thing to consider:
Support your simple phrases with "extras" such as...

- Change in voice tone and inflection to catch their attention
- Stop and sit for a second and look them in the eye
- Simple visuals (like pictures of routines or how they should act)
- Repetition
- Rhyming
- Gestures

Add all of these things so you can avoid adding *more words!*

ACTION STEP: Think about a time recently when your kids heard a long speech from you. Did you speak in paragraphs or word by word? Write out your lecture as best you can remember. Think about saying it again to them, but this time subtract words by adding in more pauses between every set of three to five words, more tone, more gestures, more sign language, more drawing, and more key phrases. How could changing the format of how you speak change the outcome of your lecture? Hopefully you will find that it becomes more meaningful, has more clarity, and has more consistency. This is the kind of direction and connection a child is begging you to have.

RULES BRING CALM TO CHAOS

If you don't know the rules, how can you expect your kids to know them?

A client of mine called me to ask if I would come to observe her family's hectic and horrible morning interactions. I got there early to start the observation. In fact, it was so early that the lights of the house were not on yet. Mom came to the door in pajamas and I entered the house where everyone else was sleeping. I stayed downstairs but could hear the goings on that were happening as she went upstairs to try to wake the kiddos. Her husband was home too and he joined in the corralling that eventually got them all downstairs, but not without a lot of yelling, screaming, and whining.

Next up was gathering things, grabbing a bite, and last-minute touch-ups to hair, teeth, and backpacks. In the midst, kids were crying, fussing, and throwing a few hurtful punches and words each other's way. To say the least, the mom was right—it was downright horrible and hectic. They were late for the bus because of the fuss and Mom and Dad flew out the door to get them down the street. I stayed back and wrote these four words at the top of my page of notes: WHAT ARE THE RULES?

Throughout my observation, I was trying to figure out what the family morning time rules were. It was hard for me to tell with all the chaos, so when Mom and Dad reentered the house and we sat together at their kitchen table, I asked. They looked at each other with furrowed brows and said, "We have no idea." And I said, "Wow, if the author of the rules don't know the rules, then how can we expect the followers to know the rules?"

The first step is always to know your rules. If you find a certain part of your day, interaction, or situation in your family running amok, step back and ask yourself, "What are the rules?" If you cannot name them, odds are your children cannot either.

These rules provide the system or conveyor belt of your day. When you follow along with them, the whole system follows along too. Of course there will be bumps but the system gets your team back on track.

The golden ticket of parenting has three parts:

1. Decide on your rules, systems, boundaries, expectations, and Go Behaviors and *teach* them.
2. Model them.
3. Practice them and praise them when you see them in action.

You cannot teach, model, practice, or praise what you do not know. So take time to decide what the rules are in your house. What will you put up with and what will you not put up with? How do we act at the table, how do we follow the wake-up steps, what do we do first, second, third, and how do we ask for things? There are so many small things that need to be taught that it can seem overwhelming, but if you don't stop the conveyor belt to set it up correctly, it gets a little more wild and unruly.

Rules help kids feel like their life is predictable and safe and although they might balk at first, they will follow along knowing they can count on those rules to be there day after day. My three simple rules in all situations are: No Hurting, No Fussing, and No Disrespect. These are general enough that they cover everything. I also would include rules at the table, rules for schedules, rules for car behavior, and boundaries and rules that help them walk through the small moments of the day and keep the family on track.

What are your rules?

ACTION STEP: Write the rules down as if a babysitter was taking over for the day. What would they need to know about how we act at your house? Keep it simple, just a few rules per situation. Set the rules and order so everyone feels safe. What are your zero tolerance rules?

KNOW AND SHOW THE GO BEHAVIORS

Put your energy into the Go Behaviors that help your child grow.

Earlier we discussed Stop Behaviors—all those things that halt the day and make it go sideways. Stop Behaviors are obnoxious, bothersome, loud, annoying, hurtful, and disrespectful. They are the behaviors that make us turn the car around and stop the day and pack our bags and leave the visit to the museum. They stop the fun and ruin the function of our day.

Go Behaviors do the complete opposite. **Go Behaviors are functional, friendly, recovery-oriented, peacemaking, productive, and playful.** They don't stop the day, they help us stay and play and function with others in our family and friend group. We've discussed ways to make this happen by taking time to decide what we want the Go Behaviors (or systems and rules) to be. We also discussed how to teach children about how to do those behaviors and how those behaviors can change the outcome of their day.

I usually bring this up in my speeches to parents by having them first list the Stop Behaviors that they'd wish would vanish from their child's life.

I met with one parent recently who told me the one Stop Behavior they'd like to see go away was snarkiness. This mom knew exactly what she meant by this, but I wasn't exactly sure. Snarky is an adjective, not a verb, and behaviors are verbs or actions, so I tried to get more details. Where do you see snarky? When do you see snarky? What does snarky look like? This is where we get to the active behavior. The mom said she sees her daughter mocking her, negotiating with her dad, being impolite to adults, and using a disrespectful tone. Here is where we started to get to the real-life behaviors and beyond the adjectives and character traits.

So we cut them down to simple terms: mocking, negotiating, and impolite words and actions. I needed a little more info so Mom said an example was interrupting and using a disrespectful tone, typically while huffing and puffing. I asked Mom to decide which of these was standing the most in the way of her child's function. She said negotiating. So we paused there. I asked her in those settings where she negotiates, what do you wish your child would do instead?

"I wish she would just do what I asked."

I returned, "It sounds like she doesn't like what you are asking her to do."

So we needed to give her some new responses that allowed the child to have her opinion and still meet Mom in the middle. We needed to find the middle between negotiating out of doing what she needs to do and doing them perfectly.

I needed Mom to think through the steps of how these situations could go:

1. Mom makes a request.
2. Child doesn't like it.
3. Child says aloud, "I do not like it." She is sharing feelings in grown-up ways without arguing.
4. Mom says, "I hear you." She's trying to meet in the middle.
5. Child gets one chance to voice an adjustment—one chance.
6. Mom gets one chance to come closer to the middle.

Suddenly we had a new Go Behavior plan. We even had terms around it—share feelings, one chance for change, and come closer. These were appropriate and mature negotiating tools. We could teach the child these skills and this pattern. We could encourage Mom to do her part in this process and practice it before she has to teach it to the child.

Whatever the Stop Behavior is, there is probably an opposite behavior that can be taught, modeled, practiced, and then praised when it shows up. These opposite replacement behaviors are Go Behaviors because they help the child go through their day more successfully. Teaching around them, naming them, and walking through them via role-play and practice helps them come to life.

Assume they don't know how else to react and it's our job to teach them new ways to respond in the same old situation. Notice we didn't change our expectations, they are still going to come towards us and do what they are expected to do, they just have a voice and choice within it and you don't have to be as forceful and disconnected with it because they are vested in the plan.

ACTION STEP: Put a name on the Go Behavior. Give it a fresh look and fresh term to support exactly what it is. By stating aloud what you expect, by teaching, modeling, and practicing it with the exact new wording or actions you would like them to do instead, you can begin to help them know exactly what to do instead. The Lord told us to say what you need. Name it to claim it.

BIBLE VERSE: "Have faith in God. Truly I say to you, whoever says to this mountain, be taken up and cast into the sea, and does not doubt in his heart, but believes that what he says is going to happen, it will be granted him. Therefore, I say to you, all things for which you pray and ask, believe that you have received them, and they will be granted you" (Mark 11:22-24).

WHEN IN DOUBT, DRAW IT OUT

The next crucial step in the teaching process is modeling.

Parents will often say to me, "Oh we've taught this to our kids, but they just aren't listening or simply aren't doing it." And I usually share a story with them about when I was a preservice teacher still in college and trying to learn and practice how to teach. We were out in the field during our senior year student teaching practicum. We had learned all the theory and now it was time to put it into action, but when we got out there, those cookie-cutter approaches to teaching weren't working exactly how we intended. We'd come to our seminar with our course instructor in the evenings after teaching all day and tell her something must be wrong with the kids. And she would shake her head and say, "It's always you. **It's never the kid.** There is something wrong with the way you are teaching."

She helped me to see that I was the "adult" in the room. I was the one with the power to change my approach. If my current way was not working, then I should tweak it and adjust based on the way the child learns. She said to follow the child. What I found was that I was talking too much and not showing enough. The showing was missing because I assumed (wrongly) that my students were wordsmiths, but kids are not wordsmiths like adults are. They can get lost in our descriptions or caught up in the vocabulary and steps. They need to see it and live it, not just hear it. My professor was right—it was me that needed to change, not the kids.

When your kids were little you probably noticed they loved a good picture book to teach a lesson or tell an example of how to do something. Our tech-heavy world has made visual learning paramount, so add it to your parenting approach.

When you sit down together (outside the moment) to have your teachable moments, pull out a piece of paper (in fact, I suggest buying a sketchbook for your kids) so that you can put your visual descriptions and conversations into one place where you can revisit them when your child needs a refresher. This paper between you will become a buffer. Instead of looking directly at your child, you can look to the paper and draw out the scene, list the ideas, or create a flow chart of options and steps. The paper becomes the problem and together you look to the paper to solve it instead of pointing with words and fingers towards the child and lecturing them with paragraphs of words trying to get them to own the problem and fix it. We can use the paper as our model and help the child to not only hear the solutions, but draw them up with us, add to them on the spot, and then see them come to life ahead of time.

Some examples of drawing it out that I have done with students and parents with their children include:

- Acting it out through role-play with characters or with each other (visually depicting how a new response can happen).
- Drawing out a situation and having your child add to it and then redraw it to show the flexible new approach that changes the outcomes.
- Choice and consequence charts that show what they can choose, what they choose as a follow up, and how those choices influence their day.
- Showing a situation from another person's vantage point.
- Posting the rules, the steps, or the expected routines and key phrases.

Draw out and highlight the cues, codes, and systems that you will be using to help them turn their behavior around. Teachers usually have their rules posted and they often role-play how things will take place before they actually take place. You can take a cue from teachers and when in doubt, draw it out if you want your children to really know how to go about their day.

ACTION STEP: Post the rules, refer to them, and let them be the bad guys around the house saying, "Look, the rules say..." Have your child be a part of the design and listing of rules so that they feel like they are part of the decision-making process. Little kids will often go to the rules and show you how they broke them. You can also post the next steps or consequences of rules so that kids can clearly see what will happen as a next step.

CONTINUOUS PRACTICE

When kids learn a new skill, they need time to practice and mess up as they learn to refine that skill and make it better. Create a safe space to mess up and allow lots of practice.

Your child's outbursts in public can make you want to pull your hair out and run for the hills. They put you and your spouse on high alert and can even cause you to win enemies (the people sitting next to you at church) and lose your friends (the parents of the kid your child bit at storytime).

The truth is you can't avoid going to the grocery store, visiting the library for storytime, or going to restaurants forever. If you *do* avoid them, how will your child ever learn to do it right? If you are struggling with some kind of public display of bad behavior, start by practicing the skills they need at home. Here are some ideas to get you started:

Practice Make Believe Style

- Practice at your dinner table or play table near your kid-size kitchen. Let them have a chance as the waitress and give them a "show" of what not to do. Then talk about the rules for the restaurant table.
- Practice going to storytime by hosting a storytime for your child and all their stuffed animals. Let Daddy play the part of the disruptive kid and then talk about the rules for storytime.
- Practice how to go to the grocery store by setting up a model store with your play grocery cart and food. Go through what are Stop and Go Behaviors for the grocery store.

Preview the New Expectations and Replacement Behaviors

- Before you get to where you are going, read through a list of dos and don'ts and add in pictures so they can see it and hear it.
- Give them the steps for what will happen if things don't go well.
- Give them certain cue words that you will say when you want to get their attention in the moment.

Real Life Practice—Celebrate Small Bits of Progress

- Choose a time when you can go with one child at a time so they get the individual attention they need to learn these public behaviors, without the siblings around to heighten the stress.
- Plan on a visit that will be short and sweet so that you can ensure more success.
- Don't make it a high-stakes visit to the store or fancy restaurant. Start small with a quick trip to a joint that is kid-friendly so that your child can gain incremental successes and you can begin to believe they can succeed at this.

Remember They Are Still Growing

- Notice the positives and go back to the drawing board with the negatives (remember these are not trouble, just teachable).
- Go home and acknowledge how well they did with certain things.
- Give them more practice and redo your consequences or next steps if things aren't working or if they need some follow-through to help them see that you mean it. They have to behave better in public.

All this practice won't make your next outing perfect, but it might make it a little easier. It will set your child on track to continual improvement and that just means more family function and fun!

ACTION STEP: The examples in this summary are more for little kids, but take time to think about how you could incorporate practice into your big kids' lives too. Role-play conversations that they hope to have with their friends. Talk to them about how they behave around you and their siblings is how they are likely to behave around their friends. Hold them accountable for what you've practiced so that they can show you that they are capable of leaving the home and participating in the things they want to do. Kids who can't show success and sincere respect for their family in their home life are kids who might have to miss out on their social life. Don't be afraid to let the natural consequences here step in and do the job. Expect the best, teach the best, model the best, and practice to help them attain the best version of themselves all so that they can go out there and be the best friend, student, customer, or leader they can be with others outside of the home.

Part Five

Top Tips

TECH—THE LAST RESORT

Get a handle on the Tech Takeover.

When you look through your child's holiday wish list, do you see mostly technology toys?

Devices
Video Games
Gaming Systems
Tablets
Laptops
Phones
iTunes gift cards
Cameras

Adding in more technology may end up subtracting more from your family time. Don't let technology rob your family of crucial teachable, positive growth moments that involve people-to-people connections.

Keep these things in mind...

Parents Need to Model Moderate Tech Time

Avoid being on your smart phone constantly. This includes texting, constantly connecting to social media (Facebook or Instagram), and looking things up when your child is around. They are watching you, and you might be sending a signal that something else drawing your attention away from them is simply more important than what they have to say or do. I doubt that is the message you want to send them, so don't! Carve out a space to put your phone away (out of sight, out of mind) so you are fully present in their life when they need you.

Avoid being on your phone at transition times within your day. For example, at pick up or drop off from school, dinner time, or bedtime.

Just be present. *Be there* with your child, eye-to-eye, ready to hear them and connect to what they need from you. Give them the attention they crave so they don't seek attention in negative or inappropriate ways. This goes for *all kids of all ages,* especially teens. They *still* need you, especially when they come in and out of your life throughout the day. They want to reconnect but if you are busy on tech they might learn that it is not beneficial to interrupt you.

Compartmentalize your time on tech and put a solid boundary on when you yourself are on it. Let no email, phone ringtone, or text beep interrupt your conversations with your child. It can wait! This is crucial to modeling that technology is not allowed to rule the house and that parents won't choose tech over personal relationships! Also, it is not important to post, document, and share everything. We all know the wasted time spent setting up the perfect photo op (time that could be spent enjoying the moment), posting it (time that could be spent looking your kid in the eye), and rereading the responses from friends who see what you posted online. All of that is so outer world focused, meanwhile your kids just want you to be present in the picture-perfect moments of your real life. Post less, be present more.

Fill your home and their life with "anti-tech" options so they are less likely to rely on technology to entertain their brain. It is hard to have your hands on tech if you have your hands on a shovel digging out a new sandbox in the backyard. Put them to work. It is hard to have your hands on tech if you have your hands out volunteering at the local soup kitchen every Monday night with siblings and neighbors. It is hard to have your hands on tech if you are playing board games or pickleball in the backyard. Set them up for tech success by having less.

Are You Stuck on What to Buy Beyond Tech?

Take your child to the gift shops at local museums (Museum Center, Art Museum, Nature Center, or the zoo). Check out all the really cool toys, books, and gifts they have to offer. Take note of the things that your child is interested in and make sure these things fill the space under the tree on Christmas morning and birthday wish lists.

Follow their tech lead. If they love to play doll dress up games on their iPad, then buy them a real-life doll with lots of real-life buttons and snaps and crazy outfits to keep their little hands busy and their minds creating. If they like games like *Minecraft* then buy them architecture sets or real-life mini tools to build things. Kids' brains cannot truly bloom on tech experiences. To really grow in knowledge and skills they have to touch, feel, and move their bodies while they learn.

Limit tech time in general by limiting tech experiences when you are out and about. Children *do not* need to be watching TV every time they sit their tush in their car seat. They *should not* be playing on your phone every time you sit down to dinner at a restaurant. You might say, "But they have never done these parts of our day without tech and they are really bad it." Everybody starts by being really bad at new skills. Remember—teach, model, and practice to change behaviors and refine new skills. These skills are worth going through tough times to get on the other side of them. Going through the grocery store *should not* be a "total tech" experience for your child as they get sucked into games on your phone. We should use these mini parts of their day as opportunities to teach patience, creative play, and engagement with their world and the people in their family. Save tech time for a small portion of your day, not as the go-to option in all situations. If you have never tried taking your child out and about without the phone to keep them busy, this will be very tough at first, but hang in there. As you and your child get more practice, you will begin to see them grow.

Monitor Your Child's Tech Experiences

Parents need to be consistently checking in on their tweens and teens as they open themselves up to more texting, social media, and the heart ache and stress that comes from being social on the screen. I say tweens and teens because kids under twelve simply do not need access to tech without you. Kids don't need phones until they are fourteen or older.

It is not an invasion of privacy to read through your child's phone and get a heads up on what the chatter is about. Look for signs of cyberbullying, inappropriate language (from your child or their friends), and apps that encourage connections with strangers and inappropriate content.

Don't freak out or harp on what you find. Just slip the things you want them to know into your next teachable moment or crucial conversation. We want to build open conversations with our kids about the realities of the tech world they live in. It is here to stay and it is our job to teach them the boundaries around it.

If you are worried that your child is spending too much time on tech, they most likely are. Think real life first and use tech as a *last resort!*

ACTION STEP: Find out as much as you can about the new apps that are coming out daily. Use websites like www.awiredfamily.org to help you learn more. Also find ways to use tech for good by going to sites like aplatformforgood.org. Read books that help you see that tech is changing your relationships and your child's brain for the worse like the *The Big Disconnect* written by Harvard Professor Catherine Steiner-Adair. Join the Wait Until 8th Movement that helps parents connect to a community who waits until kids are ready for tech before jumping into it. Visit https://www.waituntil8th.org/ to learn more.

A MORE JOYFUL WAY TO GET THROUGH THE DAY

When kids are tuning you out, tune in by using music to get the job done.

My grown-up kids think it's funny that when I clean the house, I jam to country music. I've been doing this since they were little. They'd know when those tunes start playing, Mom's in motion to get that house cleaned. Truth be told, I can't stand cleaning. Listening to my favorite music while I clean up helps make the dreadful work of scrubbing toilets and dusting shelves less dreary.

There is something to be said for having a catchy tune to transition someone from a pleasant event, like a child playing with their toys, and move them towards a not so pleasant event, like cleaning up those toys.

Imagine how many parents through the years have leaned on that darn purple dinosaur's song about cleaning up to help them get their kids to put away their toys. I know my kids could at any moment sing that song and the many others they learned from that show they watched more than fifteen years ago. Much to my dismay, I could recite those songs by heart too. **For parents, the songs our kids come to know so well can be used to redirect their brains to fall in line and do a job in a more joyful way.**

The lesson learned is when you feel like your kids are tuning you out, tune into a catchy song to get them to listen. It doesn't have to be one from a popular kids TV show (although if it is a show they are into, it won't hurt). It could simply be any words put to a common tune. You could sing about eating vegetables to the tune of *Twinkle Twinkle*

Little Star. You could sing about making good choices to the tune of *Do You Know the Muffin Man?* You could even sing about their emotions or temper tantrums and how to calm down by coming up with a song that goes to the tune of *This Little Light of Mine.* Maybe you could even get your kids on board to help you come up with a song. Whatever works, it is worth a shot to add singing to your parenting toolbox.

Singing might help you steer clear of the heightened emotions that often make behaviors go from bad to worse. It may calm your own emotions down, keep you from talking and describing too much, and singing will most certainly put you in a less serious and more playful mood. If you are using less words, less emotion, having more fun, smiling more, and are more calm, you are way more likely to get your child's attention in positive ways. So if singing can help you do these things, let's put singing to use more often in our day-to-day parenting.

ACTION STEP: Music can change the soul's response and the message reception. Use it to change your outcomes with your children. Read 1 Samuel 16:23 to see how singing can bring relief to challenging situations.

BIBLE VERSE: "Whenever the spirit from God came on Saul, David would take up his lyre and play. Then relief would come to Saul; he would feel better, and the evil spirit would leave him" (1 Samuel 16:23).

KNOW YOUR VALUES AND STICK TO THEM

Your kids don't need to shift their values to fit in, and neither do you.

It's hard to instill a moral compass in our kids' lives when we follow what the world values. And what does the world value?

Humans Having *or* Humans Being?
Having Lots of Friends *or* Being a Friend to Many?
Having the Championship Trophy *or* Being a Good Sport?
Having the Next Best Thing *or* Being Satisfied With What You Have?
Having Access to the Best Cars, Schools, and Sports Trainers *or* Being a Lifelong Learner?

When raising your little humans, pay attention to what you really desire for your children's future. Do you want them to be Humans Having or Humans Being? It is so easy to fall in line with what the world is telling you to value. All the other parents are signing their kids up for soccer at three years old. All the other families are working like dogs so they can have fancy cars and fancy homes. All the other families are putting their kids into specialized camps to increase their academic and sports skills.

Make sure your personal values come first, not the world's values, and design your parenting goals around what matters most to you and your family. If cars and houses and trophies and elite schools and camps are what you value, then so be it. *But* if a moral compass is what you want for your children, then you have to focus your family on making good choices. They have to understand that less can be more, tiny teachable moments happen all day long, and friendship skills and good sportsmanship can lead to a fun-filled social life. These lessons are all your child needs to have a valuable human life.

ACTION STEP: Make a list of what your neighbors, friends, co-workers, or bosses value. Line up their values from top to bottom based on what they give worth to. When you look at this list determine if you might rearrange these components or add to them based on what your heart desires. I once did this at a former job I held. My employer did not value family life, but I did. Upon making this list it became clear why I simply did not fit in and why I kept bumping up against my work world and coming up with headache after headache. I also found I needed a change because of this. I did not need to change my values, only change my setting. If you feel like a friend group or community you are involved in expects you to compromise what you value, you are in the wrong community and it's time to make a change. This is hard for adults to learn and you can imagine it's the same for your children. Use this storyline and approach to help them see when it is time to change their social scene or team options.

PENNIES FOR POSITIVES

You can warm a child's whole day and warm them up for making better choices by catching them being good.

When it's freezing outside, we all have dreams of summer days spent poolside. What if we could warm up the chilly days of winter by saying or doing something kind, and teaching our children that one small good choice can melt someone's heart? If you've attended one of my group presentations, then you have probably heard me talk about "pennies in my pocket."

One of my former teaching positions was a pretty rough setting where I felt like all day long I was saying, "Stop that! You can't do that! Quit it! Enough!" I was so busy policing the bad choices that I didn't even recognize all the good things that were already happening in the classroom. My classroom aide in this setting was very wise and helped me to see that if I rewired my focus and put more of my energy into noticing the good choices, I may change the whole classroom dynamic.

I decided I needed some help in this venture, so I made up a system to train my brain to focus more on the positives. We've talked about kids needing rules and systems to help them behave, and adults do too. This was a me thing, not a kid thing. I was harping on the negative and so they continued with the negative behavior. It was me who was going to have to change if I wanted my students to change.

I would put ten pennies in my pocket and every time I noticed a positive behavior, even the smallest bit of progress (and believe me this was not an easy task), I would shift a penny to my other pocket. I had to move all ten pennies in one hour and this practice really forced me to change my approach. I was forced to find good stuff happening and overlook some of the negative behaviors in the process. I did this regularly for a month and soon my brain had a new habit. It began to focus first on what was good about my situation and then zero in on what needed fixing.

Not only was this new approach changing me, the kind words and positive feedback started to rewire my students' brains too. Many of my students had been stuck in a negative storyline where they were the central character. They acted out the expected behavior which was getting them into tons of trouble. Bad choice-making was their story and they were sticking to it.

Here's how the story would go:

> They would act up,
> I would call it out.
> They would assume this is who they are (the bad kid who acted up) and then of course they would fulfill that role in the classroom one more time.
> I would call them out again.
> The cycle would continue.
> This was who they were and who they had always been, so they were staying "in character."

When I started to notice positive bits of progress instead of all the bad stuff, they suddenly had a new storyline. They were getting attention for sitting quietly instead of constantly getting my attention by being called out. They began to work to catch my attention in new and positive ways and the whole class dynamic began to shift.

One kind word or positive affirmation changed their whole day. It warmed our classroom and we began to settle into a whole new dynamic. Try catching your child when they are "doing it right." I know throughout their day there has to be a few times when they are making good choices. **So notice these moments more than you notice the bad and maybe you will warm up your whole house!**

ACTION STEP: You can pass this positive focus on to your kids too and have them start to point out what their siblings are doing right. We call it "tootling" at our house, when we tootle instead of tattle and toot our brother or sister's horn!

YOU'RE HIRED!

Get to work getting your kids to work.

During a recent one-on-one coaching session, we were dealing with a little guy who wanted lots of attention and power around his house. Mom and Dad were feeling the attention that was negative and it kept repeating until they shifted their attention to catching him being good. Yeah, Mom and Dad! Action plan one accomplished.

However, they were still struggling with behaviors and it usually showed up when they were busy doing their Mom and Dad "work." He wanted attention and they were too busy working around the house to give it to him. We decided that this little guy was like his mom and dad in many ways, including his need to stay busy and feel purpose. So we hired him!

We've all been there. Your child wants your attention and you have a laundry list of things that you *have* to get done. Kids love work and these moments are the best chance you can get to kill two birds with one stone. Involve your child in your work. They will get the attention and purpose they crave and they may even learn a few new skills along the way.

Remember these tips when doling out work:

You have to make the work involve choice where the child gets to choose what they do.

> Do you want to shred Mommy's mail after I go through it?
> Do you want to be my delivery boy and walk all the laundry to the bedrooms?

He might say neither, so you can say, "I am doing my Mommy work *(pause)* and you can help me *(pause)*. If you come up with an idea of how you can, *(pause)* let me know *(pause)*. Otherwise, I will let you know *(pause)* when I am done *(pause)* so we can do something together."

Then get busy doing a little more of your work. Maybe he will come towards you and you can say, "Are you ready to choose something to do to help or do you just want to be near me?" If he stays near you, involve him in your thought process or engage with him while you work.

You can't expect him to wait forever. Chunk your work so you can take a pausing break in the middle and try to reconnect, offering him another job or taking five minutes to connect (read a book, play a little with Legos, help him set up a racetrack).

If you put him to work, be sure not to be too critical or expect perfection. Kids will do work that mirrors their skill and developmental level of understanding. Know that with each new job experience, they will make little bits of progress. But this will not happen overnight. Make sure to add in the positive specialized attention time too, to balance out their need to play and work. Make the work pretend or silly and you will be more likely to get a positive response from your child.

Giving kids mini jobs helps them in their search for purpose, attention, and power. They get to control their day, act like a big person who is important and needed, and you get a chance to give them positive feedback on how they are doing.

ACTION STEP: Speaking of jobs, when your kiddo comes to you and says they are bored (which they are likely to do once you've limited the screen time and thinned out an overactive schedule), make a list of "Bored Chores." Home life is so busy, there really is no room for anyone to be bored. I like to send them straight to this list—clean a toilet, scrub a floor, rake a leaf. Get to work or get creative and find something else to do. Boredom is such a great thing for kids' brains, so don't be afraid of boredom. Ward it off by giving a list of chores to do if they complain about being bored. Suddenly they might get busy inventing the next best thing to keep themselves busy.

A CONSTANT MESS

No matter what, love shows up.

A friend of ours is a writer. He was doing a piece on love and asked Toby and I to contribute our own perspectives on the question: What is love?

Hearing this question was a true blessing because it allowed us to see the connections between the love we have as parents and the love shown by God at Christmas. So I want to share my shot at the question, summing it up in two main truths:

LOVE IS. . . Saying Yes to the Mess

Do you remember *The Velveteen Rabbit*? The worn and torn-up plush bunny realizes that being loved means being a little shabby.

Well, in the story of Christmas, God shows up with love in hand at the shabbiest of places. He chooses a simple young girl to be his vessel to house His Saving Son. This child arrives in a sticky and messy situation with a confused husband-to-be and questions all around. And of course that manger scene. It couldn't be messier.

All these things were God's version of true love. It was one giant mess of a situation, but Mary said yes to it. I wonder sometimes: How did she do it? She must have turned her focus on the little bundle of love that sat right smack dab in the middle of it in order to get through. She did not focus on the dirt and the crowded stable, she had to focus on what mattered most and that was the love and her faith in God's support along the way.

Raising children is a messy business, especially during the holidays. Sticky tabletops and crunched up pieces of cookie on the floor of your car. Just think about what your Christmas morning living room will look like, not to mention all the messy sibling squabbles you are going to have to deal with over winter break, and what about all the sick kids at your house?

Oh, the mess!

But here's the deal: You've said yes to all this. You've made the choice to enter into the messiest of lives and you can do it with joy and peace and understanding so it can be the greatest version of love. Hang tight through the mess, letting it go a little. Try focusing on the love that sits right smack dab in the middle of it, and keep in mind that your children are growing and learning and need your support along the way.

LOVE IS . . . A Constant That Cannot Be Undone

Just like The Velveteen Rabbit learned, once you're real you will always be real. Once love shows up it does not shift or change. God again shows us this through Christmas. There is no give and take of *His* love, it is all give and we continue to be the recipient of this love year after year no matter what. *No matter what!* That little phrase means so much and helps to show love in that steady constant stream that does not ebb or flow with negative or positive emotion, but stays the course and never ends.

This kind of love is the same we have for our own children. Yes of course there are behaviors and situations surrounding our children that we *cannot stand,* but the love part, it stays steady. You cannot change it. It isn't an emotion that runs high or low depending on the moment. It is long living, never changing, and just there, *no matter what.* Knowing this helps us keep our emotions at bay and helps us to deal more matter-of-factly with the ups and downs that come our way.

So that's it. Love is a constant and love is a mess.

You might be saying, "Love is a constant mess."

I say, "I'll take it!"

Although things will shift from toddlers with sticky fingers to teenagers with sticky situations, the mess goes on. I will keep steady keeping my emotions in check and knowing that I love them no matter what, just as God has shown me His love through the gifts of Christmas that go on and on.

Through my family's growing years, my house will not be perfectly clean, my bank account will not be perfectly overflowing, and my nights will be a little more sleepless. These things shall pass and I will survive. But the steady stream of love and learning that we pass on to our children will go on and on, reaching into the far depths of our family's future.

Know that I hope to constantly be here for you as a source of support as you work through your family's messy growing years. Hopefully I can help you through my own experiences and ideas to make the most of the inevitable mess.

ACTION STEP: Now it's time for reflection. Think about how you love your kids no matter what. How can you clearly articulate to your children that you love them no matter what, despite all the messes they bring with them?

THE BIG LITTLE MOMENTS OF OUR DAYS

Why is it that the smallest parts of our day have the potential to lead to the biggest meltdowns?

Moving from bed to getting dressed.
Moving from breakfast to packing up backpacks.
Moving from car to preschool drop off.
Moving from TV off to homework time.
Moving from playtime in the backyard to dinner. . .
Where is your biggest meltdown?

It is very likely that it is happening during the time between events, or the *transitions.* Teachers are masters of transitions. They count them as some of the most important parts of their day and they plan accordingly. They know that a poorly designed transition can lead to a failed lesson.

These little transition moments should be short lived. Yet they tend to be the sticking points where kids put up a fight and whittle your time away. If you find yourself taking too much time correcting behaviors between events in your day, transition issues are probably the culprit.

Here are some quick transition tips to make them positive, teachable moments. Within each transition:

- **Pause** before you head into the next event.
- **Review** the previous scene (positively and negatively).
  "Even though you were upset last night before bed, you fell asleep and slept all night!"
- **Connect** with your child (hug, pat on the back, listening ear).

"Can I snuggle a little in your bed with you before you have to get up?"

- **Fast Forward/Preview** (setting up the agenda, expectations, and boundaries).
  "Okay, we are going to head to breakfast. I will work on getting it ready and you will work on getting your clothes on and be at the table by the time the food is ready."
  "Remember my car is leaving at 8:30 so if you are not ready for school you will come as you are, clothes or no clothes, breakfast or no breakfast."

Some other pointers are:

- **Remind them that you've seen them succeed before.**
  "I was so excited to see you come down the stairs yesterday just as I was putting your oatmeal on the table. You are really getting good at this."

- **Give space for grace and choice without *hovering*.**
  "You will need a short-sleeved shirt and long pants, you choose something that fits those rules or I can choose for you."
  "I wonder if you will meet me at the top of the stairs when you are ready or surprise me at the kitchen table when I least expect it."
  "I will head downstairs and not bother you while you make your choice and do your job."
  Always give a "You do ______ while I do _______" statement to help you avoid too much parent controlling/lingering/hovering.

- **Preview the agenda ahead.**
  First we will_______, second_______, third_______.

- **Use visuals** to lay out the storyline, agenda, rules, and a checklist of items to do.

- **Use simple or less language and more clear cue words.**
  "First clothes, second meet me at the table, third pack up to go."

- **Avoid Please?, Okay?, or Yes or No questions.**
  They make kids think that all this is optional.

- **Positives, Positives, Positives.**
  Avoid too much gushy positive, just use simple "I noticed" statements.

- **Offer a well-placed "help" or a well-placed yes.**
  These are special because you are helping or saying yes with something you usually say no to.
  "Can I help you do that today because I know you are running a little behind?" (This makes your help special and not all the time.)
  "Mom can I have an extra cup of juice this morning?" "Yes, I know how fast you were running around to get ready so quickly."

- **Add fun and excitement to the transition.**
  Play music on the radio in the kitchen as you clean up your plates.
  Race to the top of the stairs like bunny rabbits.
  Count off like a rocket ship as you buckle them into their seat belts and head on your way.

ACTION STEP: WOW! That's a lot of stuff to jam-pack into a tiny little transition time! So just try one new thing from this list of ideas. Add it in consistently before adding in another idea. Soon your transitions will run much more smoothly, and you will avoid wasting all that time coaxing them from one event to the next.

NO MORE WHY

Stop asking why and start asking what.

Your ten year old crashed her bike into your new car.
Your toddler threw his toy at the puppy.
Your son whacked his sister over the head with his toy train.
And you say, "Why in the world did you do that?"

This question assumes your child was thinking, and odds are there was no thinking going on at all.

We use this phrase to get more information but all we end up getting is more headache. I guess we assume this phrase will cut the perpetrator some slack, let him have his chance to tell his side of the story, or help him come up with a good excuse for being nasty. By opening up the conversation with questions about the child's "thought process," we set ourselves an emotional debate.

Let's think this through. Is it debatable that his brother deserved a whack over the head? Maybe. *But* if we stick to the *what,* we can focus on the behavior and not the emotions that caused the behavior. Simply put, "We don't hit," even if our brother annoys us. There is no need for you to focus on *why* he did it. If we really want to know why they did it, simply ask more *what* questions instead of delving into the *why*. The *what* questions will yield more of the info you need as they help you gather the facts.

Start with these fact collecting questions :

- *What* happened (to your brother, to the car, to the puppy)?
- *What* happened first, second, and third?
- *What* happened just before?

- *What* happened just after?
- *What* were you feeling just before?
- *What* were you feeling just after?
- *What* else could you have done when you feel ______?
- *What* are the house rules?
- *What* can you do to show you are sorry?
- *What* are you going to do next time?

Why questions lead to excuses, emotions, tattling, debate, finger pointing, and zero resolution of behavior.

They also lead to way too much conversation and we lose our children in the language. Parents and children may end up fussing and screaming at each other and a second layer of yuck enters the scene. When you stick to the *what* questions, it helps the parents work through this without getting accusatory and emotional. They state in a matter-of-fact kind of way:

"I love you, I can't stand what you did" (to your brother, the car, the puppy).

It also allows parents a chance to actually hear the child and may help you pause enough to hear all sides and perspectives of the story. **The *what* questions lead to the facts, the problems, the solutions, the alternatives, and they help our kids learn to rewind, restart, and regulate their choices which might help them when this situation arises again.** And unfortunately we all know it will arise again. Remember they're growing and so are we.

ACTION STEP: The following three questions are questions to omit from your vocabulary: "Why did you do that?" "What were you thinking?" "What's your problem?" All three of them are highly emotional and bring up all the reasons a person might make a poor choice and there are always good reasons for doing bad things. Think like a detective and avoid *why*. A detective who enters a crime scene would never ask, "Why did you rob the bank?" Obviously the person probably has a good reason (for example, maybe he needs to pay his bills). Instead the police would try to ask facts first: Who, what, when, and how.

STEP UP YOUR TIME-OUT STRATEGIES

If it ain't broke then don't fix it.
If it is broke it ain't working so try something new.

What is your current method for dealing with poor behavior choices? If you kids are young, odds are it involves some form of time-out. When we look up what the definition of a time-out is we find this: *Time-out is a technique in which a child is removed from activity and forced to sit alone for a few minutes in order to calm down.*

Time-out is usually a punishment or consequence surrounded by negative emotions, words, and actions. It usually involves isolation for a set time and it is always designed and controlled by the parent. *If* time-out is working, you will know because your child won't have to go there *all* day every day. If instead you are finding that every fifteen minutes you are dragging your child to time-out only to have him turn around and do it all again, *it's not working!* I really can't say this enough.

If your current method of dealing with behaviors is not working, then try something else!

It has been my experience that time-out (as described above) works best if we include it as *one* of the set steps within our "Consequence Continuum." Time-out cannot be the end-all be-all of your behavior modification plan.

So what other steps should you have on this Consequence Continuum? My theory is that we need our kids to begin to regulate self and this needs to be our *main* concern. This means that they will begin to recognize what is not working for them, think about choices, and get themselves together on their own without us dragging them through the time-out shenanigans all day every day.

Here are some quick steps to include in your Consequence Continuum where they are not in trouble, just in the midst of trying again and trying to learn:

1. Give them chances to get it together before we drag them to time-out.
2. Help them come up with alterative choices for dealing with their world.
3. Preview and teach the new choices through modeling and reminding.
4. Give them practice making better choices in successful small increments of time.
5. Let them rewind so they can do it better, say it nicer, or try it another way.
6. Offer a chance to pause and take a break so that they can calm on their own.
7. Choose zones or activities that encourage calming and regrouping. Try to make the take a break zone include choices and a spot that is different than time-out. Because time-out *has* usually been a punishment, take a break zone has to be more positive.
8. Allow your child a chance to come out of break when they are ready to rejoin the social scene.
9. If they just can't get it together, or if they have done something that is off the charts bad, then they will have to go to a time-out, where they are firmly escorted and they take a loss.

Having layers or steps in your plan will allow the child to taste the sweet success of self-control and regulation more often and avoid the defeat of regular time-out punishment. It allows parents more opportunities to catch their child being good and a chance to tell their child that they noticed that they are growing in their self-control.

Remember in all these, it is *the child* who has made a choice to go there by choosing the negative behavior. This takes the pressure off of the parent and it releases some of the emotion tied to consequences. You love them, you just don't love the behavior and their behavior has led them to the consequence. If you choose to make a poor choice over and over again, you have chosen to go to time-out. If you choose to get it together through the PREVIEW, REWIND, or TAKE A BREAK steps, then you have chosen to avoid time-out.

Hopefully your child will see this play out consistently from you and they will begin to see that getting it together on their own through the first steps is much easier to deal with than going to time-out all day every day.

ACTION STEP: The top four consequences I like to give to children are simply next steps. As a next step, they can pause and take a break. This is not trouble, not timed, and they can come back when they are ready. They can fast forward and look ahead and get themselves together for the next moment of their day. They can rewind and try again all without getting in trouble, while showing parents that they can self-regulate and get back to having fun and function in their day. Add one of these consequences to you day and see how it changes your child's outcomes.

CAUTION: DON'T FEED THE MONSTERS

Don't give energy and sustenance to your child's out of line behavior.

Do you have monster-like behavior lurking in your house? Whining, screaming, gnawing at your emotions and patience? Like any monster, in order to survive, this behavior has to be fed a daily dose of sustenance. What are you giving to your child's behavior that helps it survive? Is it a dollop of good old-fashioned attention that feeds the wild beast? Is it your emotional reaction that this behavior gobbles down and then begs for more? Is it conversation and debate that helps this behavior linger around your dinner table a little longer?

How do we put an end to the monster behaviors and replace them with civilized, well-mannered, regulated princes and princesses?

First: In order to put an end to the monster we need to name it. I don't mean calling it Godzilla, King Kong, or Snuffleluphagus. We just need to say what *it* is: biting, pushing, talking back, arguing, tantrumming, or refusal to do something. If we don't name it, we can't get rid of it.

Second: Once your monster has a name, you need to go on the search for this behavior around your house and throughout your day. This is a bold and scary step, but you can't take care of a monster until you know where or when it shows up and find the patterns to the behavior. So be on the lookout for monster behavior hiding in the shadows of your day.

Third: When you see the monster, stop feeding it. That means stop talking so much, stop the back and forth tug of war which monsters love to compete in, stop reacting to the monster with shrugs, screams, or emotional breakdowns. Monsters can only survive when you feed them. Start to be aware of how you as the parent might be contributing to the life of the behavior.

Fourth: Visualize peace in your kingdom and decide what you would like to replace the monster behavior with—sharing, caring, using words, or kind actions—and then train your monster on how to replace the yucky behavior with more appropriate behavior. What would you like to see more of? And how can you teach them how to do it right?

Fifth: When a little prince or princess shows up, feed them with positive reinforcement. Let your kids know that you would like to see more of the positive behaviors in your kingdom and do this by saying a quick, "I noticed. . ." sentence.

Follow these steps and you will begin to turn this scary script into a fairy tale.

Quick Tips for Monster Slayers:

- Give them the tools and practice they need to learn to take a break and melt away their monster emotions.
- Lay out the procedures for what will happen when they just can't pull it together (will they take a break, take a loss, or take a time-out?)
- Preview that monster behaviors are zero tolerance: no hurting, no fussing, no disrespect.
- Remind them that nice gets nice and nasty gets nothing: no attention, no emotion, no drama.
- Give them chances to rewind and say something or do something in a more royal fashion.
- Give them opportunities to take a break and rejoin the social scene when they are ready to be nice.
- Take a break yourself when you need it and pause before you enter into the monster's territory.
- Walk away and tell them to let you know when they're ready to

make a better choice. Don't engage a monster!

- Take yourself out of the storyline. Let them be the character in this story so that they can be in charge of how it ends.
- Make a vow to stop feeding the monsters in your house and you will find that your home is filled with *way* more treats and a lot less tricks!

ACTION STEP: It is okay to name and number the bad behaviors that our children are displaying. Numbering means counting the where and when and how many times a day this is happening. Remember it is just behavior. In the world of behavior management within school settings, we know we first have to *look* for the behaviors, then see what happens *before* and *after* the behaviors. Then, we can see what we can change from our angle to help the child adjust the behavior. Naming it is crucial. Changing our before and after is the second step. Then, if we did a good job of naming and numbering the behavior, we can see that what we are doing around the behavior is changing it. These changes help us feel better about the support we are giving our child.

FLAILING NOT FAILING

Let go and let them flail so that God's grace can give them the lift in life they need.

We already discussed that there is something in the suffering and sometimes as a parent we need to go through it to get to the other side of growth for our child. And sometimes we need to witness our child suffer through challenges and disappointment and hard times.

The pressure of perfection from parents to children can be a lot, especially when the child begins to feel like everything should come easy for them. **Life is filled with tough times and kids learn how to work through those times by learning the difference between flailing and failing.** I tried to tell many of the parents of my students to be okay with lesser grades or less than perfect outcomes from their child. It might be that the teachers are giving the child the challenges they need. The teacher is giving a gift to the child. That gift is a chance to become better and better at learning that life can be hard and sometimes they have to push through it and do so with a sense of resilience.

Working to learn is good for kids. It is a chance for them to rely on God more and a chance to learn that they can survive tough times because they have His power lifting them up through it. Picture a wind tunnel advertisement at a used car lot. You know, those long tubes that flap in the wind but never fall all the way to the ground? That's what experiencing flailing can do for a kid. It might seem scary to watch your child flail, but I suggest doing this while they are in grade school so that when the higher stakes of college and high school come along, they will have the resilience to push through challenges, knowing they will come out on top surviving.

Where in your child's life could you let them *flail* more? This means stepping in less, letting consequences happen naturally, removing safety nets, avoiding coddling, and catching them when they fall. This means minor suffering to learn to get themselves back up. When children face difficulties, they develop resilience and learn to persevere. This is what we call "flailing"—facing challenges head-on while continuing to move forward. It's different from failing, which implies giving up.

ACTION STEP: Consider where in your child's life you can encourage more flailing. Start small and gradually increase the level of challenge as they demonstrate resilience. This will help them build the confidence and skills they need to navigate the inevitable ups and downs of life.

MEALTIMES MATTER

This might be the shortest message in the book, but it is the most important. It's simple, clear, and to the point. Coming together for meals matters, so do it!

Although dinnertime at our house may not always run smoothly, it serves as the number one factor that ensures our family's success.

Studies show that children who sit down with their family regularly (for breakfast, lunch, or dinner) are more likely to do well in school, attain their goals, and succeed socially. This is because the family mealtime provides routine, consistency, and connection. The rules and expectations of family life are practiced at this table. Sharing and caring about each other's lives takes place here, and it's also a place to practice socially correct behaviors while trying new things in the company of those who love you *no matter what.*

If we have meals together regularly, we have better odds at having children who succeed. Even if the only time we can connect is during a late-night snack or over cereal and milk before the bus comes, *make it count.* Sit down with your kids and pause a bit.

The world is telling us that sports, activities, and work matter, but I think *we* know what *really* matters.

Making connections with our kids—*that's* what matters most.

Helping them connect the dots of their world is what these connections can do, and what better place to do this than around your dinner table? Make mealtimes matter, carve out moments around the table breaking bread and uniting as a family. If you do this regularly, you will see your family *bloom.*

ACTION STEP: If you agree that mealtime matters, or if you simply want to find out more about what research says regarding regular family meals, check out one of my favorite reads: *The Surprising Power of Family Meals* by Miriam Weinstein.

TAP IN AND OUT

Set up a code of conduct between you and your spouse or other caregivers.

You've been dealing with your kids and their behaviors all day and the straw's about to break the camel's back. Your spouse enters the room. They've heard the way the kids are talking to you and they break in to go off on the kids and get these kids in line. Pause!

At that moment, one of a few things could be happening:

1. You might be at your total wit's end, so you are begging your spouse to Tap In so you can Tap Out.
2. You might have finally come to the pivotal moment where you call your kiddo out and you don't need your spouse to come and wreck the progress you've made throughout the day. You ask your spouse to Tap Out because, although you are overwhelmed, you're Tapped In.
3. Or maybe you want to stay Tapped In and have your spouse there for reinforcement and level-headed outside perspective.

These are just a few of the scenarios and perspectives that could be taking place. Either way, it's crucial for you and your spouse to have a code. Codes are crucial for kids. They are the key words that signal to your kids exactly what's next, what's going on, and what you are feeling. They are also crucial if parents want to show a united front to their children. You can call it whatever you like, using whatever code words or signals that work naturally for you and your spouse, but without a system like Tap In and Tap Out, you and your spouse run the risk of butting heads, stepping on each other's toes, and sending mixed messages to your kids. This is pure gold for a kid who is trying to break rank—get the parents to get on each other's nerves and the focus leaves the kid and enters the adult zone. Soon Mom and Dad are busy fighting and the kid is back doing whatever the heck he wanted to do in the first place.

So between the two of you, decide your system, put it to use, and practice it. Like any new system or behavior response, teach it to each other through drawing it out (writing it down or literally drawing it out). Putting it on paper makes it real and if it is real, it will have a name and if it has a name, it is easily recognizable to each of you and more easily called upon when you need it. This kind of structure and order between you is exactly what drives a kid crazy. He can no longer play games pitting you against each other or banking on your argument to supersede his behavior. So stay on the same page and design that page together so that you can call on it and use it when you need someone to Tap In or you want to go it alone and need the other person to Tap Out.

ACTION STEP: Decide what words or gestures you are going to use to signal to your parenting partner. Make a list of environments where it is likely to show up. Then put it to use right away, even if it is not exactly necessary, just for the practice to see how it feels. Then tweak it to match what you need as you figure it out. Remember, you will be in the learning process when you first start this so one of you is bound to mess up by stepping in to correct the scene without an invitation. Don't get too upset. Pull the person aside to talk things through. Just avoid doing any arguing or discussing in front of the kids.

WHAT TO TEACH?

Every time you think of a negative response or behavior from your child that is ruining their day, it should be a signal for you to teach.

I thought I should share some examples of what to teach and how to teach so you can see the simplest of skills needed to be taught. These examples are all from one client interaction and all things the parents left with to work on via teaching. Of course they won't be able to teach all eight skills right away. So they decided to choose the most pressing issue and start there. The list of teachable items for this child included:

1. **Done Is Done:** the child needed to learn that when playtime is over, it's over.
2. **Grandma Is Leaving:** the child needed to learn how we act and how we do not act when Grandma is leaving.
3. **No Hitting, No Spitting, No Hurting:** The child needed to learn that in our home we do not hurt, and spitting can hurt by being germ-filled and gross, and hitting can hurt. The child also needed to learn what happens next after hitting or spitting (if you hit or spit, you sit).
4. **Who's In Charge of the House**
5. **First Time Listening**
6. **Play Nice**
7. **Rules of Wrestling**
8. **What Does READY Mean**

You can see that some of these items involve a code word like *ready*. We assume our kids know what we mean when we say things like "get ready," but odds are likely that they don't know exactly what we mean.

This needs to be taught, modeled, and practiced. It could mean body-ready (being regulated, relaxed, or still). It could mean materials-ready (like backpack packed, teeth brushed, or breakfast put away). Get specific with the things you need to teach your kids and don't assume they know what your words mean.

Some of these items are to teach a lesson about the home hierarchy and listening on the first time. Teaching these skills through teaching kids responses that reflect them is key. And in the case of hurting, it is important to also teach the consequences that follow.

These teachable moments would warrant a sketchbook where you can draw out the scene for the child. Draw a picture of the rules or mantra so that they can see it and hear it and therefore do it!

ACTION STEP: Make a list of your child's list of things they need to learn or hear about. Then circle one that is most pressing and focus on it, knowing that soon you will pause and teach the others.

UPON RETURN, MOVE ON

Do the opposite of what you brain says to do when they return after taking a break.

I think we can all recall a moment in our own childhood when we got in trouble, had to go to our room, and when we came out, we got a whole lecture on why we went in there and why that's not going to happen again. And in your own job of parenting, I am sure that you feel like this approach is the way you settle the score and make sure your child knows you are in charge. So you repeat the process with your own kids. It's only natural.

But the question is, does that follow up lecture really change behavior? Or are we spinning our wheels and possibly wrecking the opportunity for follow up connection or a push to move on and try again?

When I was teaching as part of a behavior unit within a school setting, I had kids who needed to take a break or take a loss throughout the day. They were constantly working on behaviors and therefore constantly messing up. I needed them to go to a calm down space that was safe and I needed them to come out of that space or break ready to enter back into our zone. Sometimes I found there was not enough time to lecture as they returned and reentered the scene. It was in those times that I felt like the kids were more likely to do better. It was as if me welcoming them back, no questions asked, assuming the best, led to them presenting their best.

These kids had never been given the benefit of the doubt. They got in trouble, they got lectured, they returned to the scene, and everyone assumed they'd never get it. But what if we assumed that when they return, they know they are ready and capable of doing better. What if we showed them that we trust them and have faith in their ability to do this. What if we used minimal words to enter them into the scene? Things like:

- Thumbs up and a quick phrase, "You ready?"
- A nod and a "Welcome back."
- Or a quick question of "All Set? Good. Glad you are back."

Having these go-to quick phrases and gestures and using them regularly sets up a pattern that they mess up, as humans do, and you are there to welcome them back with your unconditional support and love. So the love acts as a sustainment to their good works. It propels them forward whereas a lecture and critique assume they didn't get it and they need to be reminded how bad they are one more time.

ACTION STEP: Release the need to lecture and give this approach a try. Ask your kids how it feels to simply get welcomed back. This can allow for more positive time to reconnect building up the relationship rather than wedging it with critique and control.

FOCUS ON RECOVERY

Put your words into acknowledging their recovery instead of reprimanding.

Once your child returns from taking a break or taking a loss, enter them back in with less words. Keep an eye on their ability to recover and join back into the scene after they've had to leave and get themselves together. If you feel the need to connect to them, connect positively about the fact that they showed you they can regulate. They were probably upset before, during, and maybe after their time-out or break, but they pulled themselves together to rejoin the fun. This pulling of yourself together takes skills that are not easy to gain. So if you see your child doing this, it is definitely worth noting.

Name it as surviving or recovering so that they see it as an entity all to itself. Naming recovery as an important part of the process of getting along in your world will help them to name it as they do it and think about the things they do to help them self-recover.

In fact, later in the day, I might even probe them to find out how they did it, saying, "Wow, you were really upset before you took a break from the game. I saw you go there screaming and yelling and then minutes later you left and came back ready to join the fun. I noticed your resilience and ability to bounce back. It was impressive. I am proud of you and I see you growing. This is who you are—resilient and recovery-focused."

I hope this acknowledgement will solidify who they are to themselves and make them see that they are capable of turning it on and turning it off. My experience with this has shown that **the more we focus on recovery, the more confident in recovery a child becomes** and the temper tantrums become less intense. If they go to a room to calm down, recovery shows up a lot quicker, little by little, the more they experience it.

ACTION STEP: If you are going to put eggs in baskets, make sure that they are in productive baskets that build change into your child's life. Recovery skills are definitely a changemaker for a kid. Consider the recovery methods above and think about how you can help introduce them into your child's life.

THE GRAY ZONE

There's always more than one way to see your day.

One of the big things that gets in the way of teaching, parenting, and being a parent who is also a teacher is the problem of seeing the word in black and white. The world is so much more than black and white. Every part of our day can be examined with a scaled approach. It is important to try to stay in the gray zone where real life happens or else we risk getting stuck in the highs and lows.

Carol Ann Tomlinson is a professor and researcher of education whose specialties include differentiating for the needs of all learners in a classroom. She used the image of a stereo equalizer to depict movement from one end of a spectrum to the other. She used this when trying to get teachers to see there were good and bad ways to ask questions but there were also many things in between these two levels and across a continuum. It reminds us that there are many ways to interact with our day and help our kids feel like they are getting what they need.

You can use the equalizer image to show that you are not asking your child to be perfect or horrible but somewhere in between. The somewhere in between are the real-life moments where things are a bit messier but the realness makes them even better than perfect.

The equalizer is dynamic, like your child, so it can adjust as the child gains more skills in these unwritten worlds. So you might want your kids to move from not getting along to being best friends and the middle zone is simply being civil (wouldn't that be nice). You might want your child to move from being shy and having trouble with friends to being a fun-loving social butterfly. There is a happy medium or just right zone where you can be a little of both. Nothing fits in a box and matches up perfectly, so it's good to help kids see they don't have to feel defeated. Other continuums with kids could be:

- Wanting to do everything ⟶ Wanting to do nothing. (There are a lot of in-between levels between these two.)
- Being angry ⟶ Being easygoing.
- Being aggressive ⟶ Being compassionate, or something in between.

Real life humans are always somewhere in between. Never perfect and never horrible. It's great for kids to think about life like this so that they can be less rigid in their thinking and better able to problem solve and progress from where they are to higher up on the chart.

ACTION STEP: Check out Carol Ann Tomlinson's book *The Differentiated Classroom: Responding to the Needs of All Learners* where you can find information and images of the great equalizer.

TALK IN YETS

Stick to a growth mindset that leaves room for what hasn't happened yet.

When we comment or discuss our kiddos and their behaviors in end-all be-all commentary, we often stifle their ability to continue to grow beyond where they are. Avoid terms like "always" and "never" or characteristics that put them in a category that is hard to bump out of.

For example, we might say, "He hasn't figured out how to turn in his papers on time." This makes the child sound incapable of doing something and it makes it seem like these lagging skills are never-ending. It's kind of a doomsday approach to supporting our kids and it poses a risk because it could mean we end up not allowing them room to grow.

So tack a "yet" onto your commentary and say, "He hasn't learned to turn in his papers on time, yet." This signals that he's purposefully working on this and it could be one of your teachable moments with him. You and he both realize there is room to grow and his abilities in this area are not fixed.

Moving from fixed to flex can help the child be more open to next steps and challenging situations. They know it is normal to not know how to do something or not be perfect at it, yet. **The "yet" gives space for time and room to grow.**

I bet as a parent or learner yourself you could even show your kids how you still have room for growth.

I could say to my kids, "I am not so good at juggling several things at once yet, but I am working on it."

I could say to husband, "I am still working on forgiveness but I'm not there yet."

The other thing to assume is that they may never reach "there," that arbitrary level of perfection. It simply doesn't exist. We are human so we are constantly learning and growing from the inevitable mistakes we will make, even when we get pretty close to mastery. If we understand the power of "yet," our setbacks can be a little easier to bounce back from because it doesn't have to be doomsday. We know we are still growing and need more time and more practice to get there.

So add a "yet" to your descriptions of your kiddos' progress and performance because they are still learning, still working on things, and still gaining skills little by little.

ACTION STEP: Check out Carol Dweck's TED Talk on the power of yet—"The power of believing that you can improve."

DROP THE ROPE

What's your current tug of war? Could you drop the rope so your child falls, only to get themselves back up again?

You say they will, they say they won't.
You say you will, they say you won't.
You say yes, they say no.
You say right now, they say never.

These power struggle tug of wars can make life with kids miserable. We as the parent think we should hold tight to a rule or procedure and our kids fight us tooth and nail. And let's be honest, their will is often stronger than ours. They are working on instinct, they haven't been here before and they are going with their gut, feelings, and emotion. You on the other hand are trying to use your adult brain with reason and analysis. So you might not dig in as deep and might question your role and authority when the child starts questioning you. So your child's powerful "no" seems like it will win.

In fact, you might just hang on and let them drag you through the mud. It's the hanging on that might get you in trouble. Holding tight to your expectations might be the thing that is keeping the power play in motion.

Have you ever watched a tug of war where one opponent drops the rope? What happens to the other person? They do that last pull and the dropped rope on your end comes flying at them as they fall to the ground. The person who drops the rope wins. The person who lets it go has the least amount of consequence. This can seem counterproductive if I am the parent trying to hold tight to my rules. But what if you dropped the fight, dropped the push and pull, and dropped the drama? You would be free.

You see, the facts are you've already been their age and you don't have to be their age again. You don't have to be in this fight. You pay the bills and author the rules. So drop the rope and stick to your rules and the next steps that follow those rules (which I hope you've already clarified by teaching, modeling, and practicing).

Dropping the rope means ending a conversation without having the last word.
Dropping the rope means stating the case (the rule and next step's consequence) and finishing there.
Dropping the rope means no drama, less words, and less expression.
Dropping the rope means allowing them to make the choice they want, but then making the next step of that choice part of the choice-making. They will feel that next step and you don't have to be emotional about it because they chose it.

It doesn't mean doing it in a harsh or hurtful way. Just stop the debate by stopping the word war. Just push pause and let the silence speak louder than the words.

Sometimes as long as they keep you in the tug of war, they feel like they are winning. So drop the rope and the war is over.

ACTION STEP: Make a list of tug of wars you've been in before and then note how you could have dropped the rope and what your "drop the rope" response might look like in that situation. Allowing yourself to walk through prior occurrences can help you see how you could use this tactic in the future.

MAKING THE BED

Allow your children to build confidence in their little achievements.

We expect our kids to be big kids, yet we end up doing everything for them. By letting your kids have more chances to do things for themselves, and do these things with success, we can hand over more power and control to them, which is all they really want. Simple things like carrying their own dish to clear the table, holding their own backpack into school, or making their own bed can be first steps to independence for them and freedom for you. Doing these things on their own without expecting them to be perfect allows them to feel like they are contributing and growing in self-help skills.

It's the low expectations of performance that is key for parents to wrap their head around. We cannot expect our kids to know how to do these things well on the first try. So give them baby steps to success and repetition with the practice so they feel repeated success before you send them on to the next level of expectation.

For example, making the bed can start out by your child fluffing their pillows and lining them up. Then once they master this and do it automatically without a cue, add in one more step like pulling up the first layer of sheet. Teach them next how to pull it up while flattening it out and let them practice these first two steps for a while before mastering the next steps of making the bed. Always add in one new skill at a time while layering the mastered skills on top of each other. What I mean by this is if they have mastered how to flatten out the sheet, then when they get to the point where they can pull up two or three layers, they will have also mastered how to flatten out each of those layers.

These little achievements build their confidence and allow for the control they are searching for. They call for mini moments of praise and the only reward needed is the feeling of accomplishment and contribution to the family system.

It's a win-win situation. We do less. They do more. And *everyone* is a little happier.

ACTION STEP: This approach has a formal name—task analysis. Basically, it is the process of breaking down an activity into smaller parts. By breaking things down into a task analysis, your child can begin to thrive at challenging endeavors. Your help in breaking the procedure down into manageable parts little by little can help them do big things. Think of a skill that your child needs to learn to improve their day and gain more independence. How can you help them attain that growth by breaking it down into doable steps, little by little?

CIRCLE OF FRIENDS: HELPING KIDS SEE THE WHOLE PICTURE

Respond in rational, not emotional, ways to help your child remain rational.

Parents have a lot of worries when their children go out to the great big world of school, playground, and sporting situations. Some of the biggest worries include wondering if their child will find a friend or if people will treat them the way they deserve to be treated. It can be heart-wrenching to have them come home only to find out they have been left out or bullied. And sometimes we rush in with our emotions. In doing so, we might risk making them feel worse, saying things like, "Well did you speak nicely to them?" "Who is it? I think I'll give that kid a piece of my mind" or "I think we need to go see a psychologist. Something must be wrong with you." All of these responses come from the depth of emotion that we are feeling in our broken heart, but they don't really heal the child's.

As a tip, I would like to suggest you go back to the drawing board, literally. Remember what we said—teach (outside the moment), model (draw it out), practice, and then praise. So in the moment, the best response can be pausing to say, "I'd like to spend time talking about this with you. Maybe now or maybe later, whenever you want to sit down and really talk it through."

This gives the child a chance to calm themselves down. It also gives them designated time focused on this particular concern. Because you are not rushing the conversation right here and now, you signal to the child that you aren't worried about them and that you want to be fully present when they are ready to have you fully present. These comments set the tone and give you and them time to prep.

When you do come together (outside the moment), you'll want to talk less and listen more. So I suggest bringing a piece of paper to the table. That paper can be a place where you take notes, writing down words that they say in their description so that you can call on those words later when you rephrase and reframe the situation back to them. It can also be a space where you draw something out to depict the situation. Drawings help to set the scene, give a visualization of hopeful remedies, and plan our next step. You might draw options, new mantras, or alternative realities so that the child can hear and see what they need in order to problem solve through this sticky situation. The drawing also brings your attention to the paper and the situation on it rather than to personalizing all this around your child. It becomes just behavior in a specific scene and not them and who they are. Finally, drawing it out and using a framework to rethink (or a graphic organizer) to help them organize their thoughts can help them see it all more clearly.

One graphic organizer I like to draw includes concentric circles patterned one after the other that look like the circles on a tree stump. The center circle is where you would put your child's name and then each circle after that is where you could put another person's initials, noting the people who are in the child's inner circle, all the way out to the edges of the shape where they would find people they know of but have no relationship with. The goal is to see that some people stay static and in place like family members and longtime friends (close to the inner circle rings), and some people might come and go along the rings as your life and experiences change.

This makes it clear that friendships are dynamic and ever-changing and what is true today might not be true tomorrow. Because the Circle of Friends includes people all the way out to the outer edges, you can always be working on bringing new people towards the center. It's also nice to draw the same kind of image for another person so your child can see that they are most likely a part of someone else's Circle of Friends.

The point is not the Circle of Friends, although it is a great way to use a visual to help when friendship woes show up. The point is the focus is drawn away from your child and towards new perspectives on a common childhood struggle. The new perspective might become the very thing that helps them realize this too shall pass. **You will be able to stay more rational and so will your child when the words are less and the drawing is more.**

ACTION STEP: What could you draw out for your child to help them bump through a tricky situation?

BABY BURSTS OF SUCCESS

Kids can't hold it together for long periods of time, so break things into tiny bursts of success.

I have a good friend whose husband is from New Zealand. Every other year when their four kids were little, they would trek across the world to visit his homeland. What a treasure of a trip! But getting there was no fun at all. That was until my friend realized that kids can't make it over the long haul. It was absolutely too much to expect from their little bodies and less refined regulation systems. She decided she would need to break the time down, for herself and her kids, into doable bursts.

So she brought a bag of bursts with her. Every thirty minutes (the length of her kids' attention spans) she'd burst out a novel item and grab their attention. This kept the excitement going and they were fully capable of keeping attentive to the items for that short burst of time. This might not be realistic to try in every situation, but it tells the story of how the parent needs to think of things in small bits of time rather than overarching blocks of time.

For instance, you are going to a birthday party and you are not sure your child will make it. What if you had a little picture schedule of the things that might happen? The schedule doesn't have to be in order, just laid out as items on a list. Then the child would go forth and experience the various short bursts of play and fun at the party (cake eating, bounce house playing, gift unwrapping, game playing, birthday singing) and you could check in, giving small bursts of praise after each small burst of function. **It is easier to tell your child to behave during the birthday song than to tell them to behave throughout the whole birthday party.** You can keep a close eye on positive behavior, note it, and then prep for the next thing on the list of things happening at the festivities.

Some teachers across the country are doing a similar approach in their classrooms. They call it the PAX Good Behavior Game and it is a research-based approach to getting through the day with positive classroom behaviors at the forefront. They start each small increment of time throughout the day by stating that, "The game is about to begin."

"It's spelling test time, the game is about to begin. It's time to move to the classroom carpet for circle time, the game is about to begin. It's the math lesson, the game is about to begin."

The game has expected and unexpected behavior based on the situation and the teacher is looking for compliance and participation from kids during a short burst of learning time. The kids are likely to succeed because the task has been broken down to a short increment of time and the teacher is likely to be more aware of successes because they have a short window of time to zero in on how kids are doing.

How could you break up a long-winded, not so successful time of your day and focus on small bursts of time on task? It may seem like all the little breaking up of time points will take more time. However, what the research shows is it actually saves time because everyone is more engaged, more productive, and happier because everyone is more likely to succeed.

ACTION STEP: Check out the PAX Good Behavior Game by visiting http://paxgoodbehaviorgame.promoteprevent.org/.

IT'S SHOW TIME!

Parents are the directors of every scene and it's okay to call for cut!

What show is playing at your house these days?

Maybe the baby in your family is running the show.
Maybe your toddler's temper tantrums resemble a horror show.
Maybe your over-the-top reactions are keeping everyone on the edge of their seats.
Maybe the sibling rivalry has turned into a violent fight scene.
Maybe your child's emotional rollercoaster is the newest drama.

Whatever show is unfolding in your home these days, it's your role as the director to make a change in order to make it go away. Each person in your home probably has a strict script that they stick to. Each child finds their niche or storyline and replays that scene over and over again because it's what gets them noticed. Even as parents we pick roles and settle into them as our comfort zone, whether they be the strict enforcer, the lenient sidekick, or the firm and consistent lead role. The first step you need to take in making a change to a negative scene is to reflect on the following questions and determine all the characters living on your set:

- What is the storyline your child has assumed in the family?
- What is your part in the drama?
- How does your part add to the storyline or take away from the sequence of events?
- Does the audience (or rest of the family) feed the negative scripts with their attention?

- Do the characters repeat their negative behaviors over and over because of the attention they receive and because they assume this is their place on the stage?
- Can you give people in your family a whole new script with specific tools to help them work through conflict?
- Can you rehearse, practice, and role-play how these new scripts will look?
- What changes could you make to help lead this storyline to a happy ending?

If you have drama happening in your home, it's not too late. You still have time to develop strong leading ladies and gentlemen who have a character sketch that includes civil and loveable behaviors. You won't win an academy award as the director of this drama, but if you begin to look carefully to see the roles everyone has assumed within your family's storyline, you will begin to see patterns of behavior. Then you can begin to design a new script that will lead to a happy ending.

ACTION STEP: Sit down and draw out the scripts that are happening (word for word) in your home. See how you could direct some changes in the environment (setting the stage for success), in your word choice (choosing your lines), and in the outcomes (the plot thickens). Seeing it on paper can help you see where you can make the biggest changes or else the story will go on and on in the same direction, night after night.

GIVE PRAISE WITH SPECIFICS

*If we want praise to be effective,
we have to be clear and specific.*

I want to be clear that using the praise phrases listed below are a great start, but they're simply not enough:

- Good job!
- Way to go!
- I am so proud of you!
- Wow, you did it!

These phrases are not enough!

You might be thinking, "Not enough? Not enough? How can that be?" Everyone has told you to be positive. What about all those trophies they've received? What about all those times you've bought them a treat? What about all those times you've told them how terrific they are?

Praising you kids is important. It's just that most praise statements are way too general. If we want the praise to be effective, we need to be clear and specific about how we praise. When we praise, we usually do so in order to change behaviors. If this is our plan, then we need to connect the praise to what they are doing or how they have specifically shown growth.

Here are some examples of how you can shift your praise from general to specific:

- Instead of "Wow!" you could say, "You tied your shoes all by yourself and no one told you to do it."

- Instead of "You're the best!" you could say, "You did your best to include your brother when your friend came over."
- Instead of "You did a fantastic job," you could say, "I saw that you cleaned up all the big stuff first and then you went around your room and gathered all the little things."
- Instead of "You are a real trooper," you could say, "I know it was hard to wait for Mommy to get off the phone, but you waited on the couch quietly and you didn't interrupt."

Adding specifics to your praise statements makes them concrete, relevant, and meaningful. It gives your child proof that you have paid attention, and they will be more likely to do things to repeat this kind of positive attention in the future.

One simple praise statement that goes a long way is, "I've noticed..." If you add a specific positive comment after this statement, it can begin to let your child know you are watching and paying attention to the good choices they are trying to make. Try to add in a few more specific praise statements into your day and watch the good choices increase. They don't need trophies, awards, special treats, or meaningless praise statements. They just need you to be specific about how their behavior matches your expectations and how you see their choices changing their day for the better.

ACTION STEP: Choose your most common general praise statement. You can ask your kids because they will probably be able to tell you what you say all the time but don't even recognize. Whatever it is, add to it by saying it like you always do and tacking on a specific phrase of what you've seen that is good.

YOU'RE SAFE

It's crucial that kids feel safe if they are going to thrive.

Your number one house rule should be "We are safe."

This is the one way to make sure that no one gets hurt or humiliated. This means that adults will not hurt or humiliate a child and children will follow suit. It also means that they will make choices that are safe.

Of course being safe means being in control of our bodies, our words, and our choices. Parents get to be the guardians of what is safe and unsafe. They have to stick to this number one rule as they practice a zero-tolerance approach to dangerous play, unsafe decisions, or harmful behavior.

Think about the things around your house and the routines in your daily schedule as you decide upon safety standards that will support this number one rule.

Use key words to show you mean what you say. "Danger!" is a great quick phrase that can let even the littlest child know that they are nearing an unsafe zone. Change the tone of your voice when you say this phrase so they can tell you mean it. Get down on their level and point to the danger item as you redirect them to another safer choice. Give them an alternate behavior to take the place of the dangerous choice.

Here is an example of what you might say: "No jumping on the couch. Danger! We can sit or lay on the couch, but we cannot jump on the couch. If we want to jump we can jump on the pile of pillows on the floor."

Here is how we could say this same statement to an even younger child in a more clear and succinct way: "Danger! No jump on couch. No, no. We can sit. We can lay on the couch. But no jump. Jump on pillows. Yes, yes. No, no jump."

Notice you gave the child a replacement space to do the thing they want to do? Practice makes perfect, so you might have to demo or role-play how to play and be safe. Tell them the story of what could happen if they were unsafe. When telling them, draw it out so they can see it, not just hear it. Talk to your child outside of the moment about these things because having an in-depth conversation in the heat of the activity will most likely be unsuccessful. They are usually not open to learning when they are excitable.

We can increase the feelings of safety by being someone they can count on and by being consistent in our tone and outcomes, following through on what we promised even if the follow through is difficult.

ACTION STEP: Think about your kids across their growing years and the differing arenas where you want them to be safe. Safe in your home, safe while driving, safe at school, safe with their word, safe with their body, safe with their choices. Choose one to teach, model, practice, and then praise them when you see them making safe choices and responses as part of their daily interactions.

DON'T GO ALL "CHICKEN LITTLE" ON US

What if your kids knew you aren't worried about them?
How would your family dynamics change?

Some say we're raising our children in The Age of Information, and who can argue with that? If we need any insights to support our parenting, it's literally at our fingertips within seconds. Like an acorn falling from the tree of knowledge, all this information can be a blessing and a curse. Maybe a better name for this generation of parenting would be The Age of Information *Anxiety*.

As parents of the new millennium, we have so much to worry about: car seats, flu shots, preschool sign-ups, IQ testing, brand names, bullying, peer pressure, screen time, perfect party planning, and more.

A quick web search on topics like the ones below could send our heads spinning and cause any parent to "go Chicken Little."

What are the effects of high-fructose corn syrup on children?

> "Help! The sky is falling, the sky is falling! I just read that I may doom my child to obesity because I allowed him to put ketchup on his broccoli to get him to eat it. What should I do? Skip the broccoli or risk obesity?"

How do I properly perform time-out procedures with toddlers?

> "Help! The sky is falling, the sky is falling! I can't get time-out to work for my child. There must be something wrong with me because it's not changing my child's behavior."

Is it ever okay to take away a child's "lovie"?

> "Help! The sky is falling, the sky is falling! Yesterday I took away my four year old's favorite bear because he's been hitting his baby brother over the head with it. Did I wreck his self-esteem forever?"

Why should we avoid too much screen time?

> "Help! The sky is falling, the sky is falling! I've been letting my youngest child watch TV while I cook dinner *every night,* and I just read that too much TV can cause ADHD! *Ahhh!*"

What are the best bets for a three year old's birthday bash?

> "Help! The sky is falling, the sky is falling! I saw the cutest ideas on Pinterest for a three year old's birthday party, but the prize baggies have to be sewn, and the cake has to be made from scratch. What will the neighbors think if I skip the homemade party and just celebrate as a family?"

The pressure is real and this is just a short list of what is coming at us. If you start searching, there are thousands of opinions, all claiming to have the answer to each parenting dilemma perfectly mastered.

Don't be fooled so easily. Don't be confused. You know who you are and what you desire and what you want to prioritize. So go there. Go back to *you* and your spouse and your kiddos because your family gets to be whoever you dream them to be, without having to be picture-perfect. **You are the one true expert on your parenting situation.**

You know exactly what you can handle and what will and will not work in your home. So don't let the internet drive you crazy. It will only add to the fear and anxiety and cloud your natural instincts.

Leave the worrying to Chicken Little and reflect on the questions below to help you figure out what matters most to you.

ACTION STEP: Take time in the silence to really pause on these questions. Listen to your inner voice and the voice of God speaking to you about what will and will not work. Once you have done some inner and spiritual reflection, your little acorn (or family) will grow into the great big oak tree it was meant to be.

- What routine parts of the day cause trouble for my kids?
- Are my partner and I on the same page with our parenting methods?
- If not, how can we meet in the middle?
- What is one new response that is doable for my family?
- What are the things that are most important to me and my spouse?
- How can I avoid getting sucked into worrying about how my parenting compares to others?
- How can I remember to catch my children being good?
- How can I encourage my child to be independent and self-regulated?
- What are the real safety concerns I need to be aware of for my child's age level?
- Can we live moderately as a family and stay afloat in this sea of information?
- What will be our family priorities?

THAT'S GOOD, THAT'S BAD

How do we help our kids to the good life?

One of my favorite children's books for helping children understand the reading comprehension concept of cause and effect is a book called *That's Good! That's Bad!* by Margery Cuyler.

In this book, a young boy starts his visit to the zoo when his parents get him a shiny red balloon. That's good, but that's bad because he is suddenly lifted high above the zoo. He loved flying high above the zoo so he could see all the animals below him. That's good, but that's bad because his balloon popped on a tall, prickly branch and he fell into a swamp. Luckily he was able to ride to shore on a roly poly hippo. That's good, but that's bad because ten baboons were fighting at the riverbank and they chased him... You get the point.

The story goes back and forth between bad and good outcomes until the boy ends up plopping back into his parents' arms when a stork carries him across the zoo. This book helps to open up a discussion with children about how each event in the story has an impact on the whole storyline. When they understand this, they begin to realize they can control the storyline in their own writing by shifting positive and negative events and outcomes.

What does this have to do with parenting?

Wouldn't it be great if we could help our children connect to the cause and effect of their behaviors and in turn, help them see that their actions affect the storyline of their day?

Here's an example:

> "Hey Mom!" said the little boy as he walked in the door after school. "I was able to go outside for recess today because I made good choices during center time."
>
> That's good, but that's bad because, "It was thirty-two degrees outside and everyone was freezing. I had a heavy coat on and was running around with my friends to keep warm. We got really excited."
>
> That's good, but that's bad because, "I got so excited that I felt like punching my friend in the stomach. I calmed down after I hit him."
>
> That's good, but that's bad because, "My friend didn't like it and he cried all the way over to the teacher. The teacher helped him feel better."
>
> That's good, but that's bad because, "When the teacher saw him crying she made me go talk to the principal, and I have to stay in from recess the rest of the week and *that's bad!*"

ACTION STEP: Helping our children experience the real-life logical consequences of their behavior can help them see that they have power in their choices and when they make positive choices, they can have the "good life." How do we help a child own up to their behavior choices and begin to make a change? Tell them the expectations upfront so they know what they are working towards. Give them a chance to rewind when they've made a poor choice. Give them a chance to take a break when they've made a poor choice and before entering back into the social scene. Have them look around and recognize what other good choice-makers are doing. These skills help children learn how to start good choice-making and stop bad choice-making.

SELF CHECK

Allow your child a chance to look at their progress.

Choose one behavior you want your child to focus on and zero in on it. For example, if you want them to practice taking turns while they play on the playground, you could remind them about this skill before you get to the playground and ask them to pay attention to how they are doing while they are playing. Then at the end of the playtime, ask them to tell you how they did. You could try to catch them being good so that you can help them remember their good choices later when they self-reflect.

They could do this self-assessment throughout:

- A simple conversation between parent and child where they tell you what went well and what did not go so well.
- A "picture storytelling" where they draw the things that went well and the things that did not go so well.
- A "fill in the blank storytelling" where you give them two prompts.

  "I took turns when I. . ."

  "I did not take turns when I. . ."

  "My friend took turns when she. . ."

  "I felt ____________ when my friend did not take turns."

- A simple smiley face chart where they color in what they did and how they felt.

- A sticker chart or some other kind of reward chart where they evaluate their progress.

Of course their perspective could be different than what really happened. This is very normal for early childhood development. They see their world differently and might need us to be specific about the good and bad choices that we saw them making. This skill takes practice for you and your child so try it more than one time before you give up.

Make self-reflection a part of your daily time together and encourage your child to reflect on their own progress as they start to own up to their behavior choices.

ACTION STEP: While you are helping your child monitor their behaviors, you could also begin to monitor your own. Start a chart to check in on how you're doing with that one new tip you want to implement. Track where you were in the beginning as a baseline, then add in your intervention and see if you can find a way to make it go away.

THE PARENT MONSTER

Monsters are lurking in your family and they are feeding off of emotional reactions and too much distraction and conflict. Set them straight.

It lays low, waiting for our children to push us to our limits. We try desperately to keep the monster hidden and out of sight, but no matter what, it creeps into our mindset and takes over our approach when we least expect it.

There's no escaping the monster when you've had a long day.

We've all had it happen. You scream like a mad woman when they've messed up your living room for the third time in one day. You roll your eyes back in your head as they tattle on their brother for the twelfth time today. Here are some quick tips for taming your Parent Monster:

1. You can love your child and despise their poor choices. Make sure your statements regarding their behavior choices are not degrading or personal. Focus on the behavior, not the child. Love them anyway. "I love you, I can't stand that your brother got hit over the head with a block." I have found that a behavior will not go away until we reach our breaking point with it and until we say we can't stand it any longer.

2. Know your limits. Set up systems that allow you to get the down time you need. Find ways for your child to play on their own, or do whatever they can independently and safely while you take a rest, regroup, or get something done. Come up with a list of safe go-to activities that give you five, ten, or thirty minutes of peace. Then go to that list when you need a break.

3. Just the facts. When you list the simple facts and avoid the fluff and circumstance, you make your tone clearer. This will help you to tame the extreme emotions that come with "heavy duty" discussions and battles of wills. Speak directly, with little emotion and simple statements, and your child will understand you better and know exactly what is going on in your mind. Here's an example:

> "Johnny, you hit your brother. Hitting hurts. We don't hurt people or things in this house. Hurting is a bad choice. Because you chose this you have also chosen to take a break from the fun (or take a loss or take a time-out)."

Avoid asking *why* or else the debate will go on and on. Just deal with the facts of what happened and how what happened doesn't match your family's plan.

4. Don't take things personally. Their behavior has nothing to do with you and everything to do with how they haven't learned to regulate or control their responses yet. You are working on getting them to do this on their own. This is a step in the right direction. It might get worse before it gets better, so take yourself out of the equation.

5. Focus on what they did well. Try to catch them in the moments where they succeeded in making good choices. This positively reinforces what you want to see and helps you to think more positively about the tiny steps of growth they are making. Focus on the good stuff.

Follow these guidelines to tame your inner Parent Monster, and hopefully your mini monster's behavior will begin to improve too.

ACTION STEP: Look around in your schedule. Where is it during your day or week when the monsters come out? Alter your schedule and routines and lean on your safety nets so you can avoid the monster or get the support you need to slay the monster.

RULES AND BOUNDARIES ARE A MUST

Let your kids take on the job of regulating their next steps naturally.

Children as young as three can think things through using "If_____ Then_____ " statements. This is called The Age of Reason, where they can judge what might happen next if they choose certain behaviors. This means at this early age, we can already guide our children to take on the job of regulating their behavior. **Having clear rules and expectations helps us help them make good choices.** Here is a summary of how you might start to incorporate your rules and expectations into your family life:

Let Children Know What Is Expected

First, state the positive expectations. When designing your house rules, make sure to consistently state the positive things you want or expect. Here are a few examples of what you might expect. Only choose three, at most, that work for your family and make sure they are general.

Be Nice.
Be Helpful.
Be Honest.
Be Gentle.
Be In Control.

Then, get specific. Start to think about what each positive expectation covers, and make sure your children understand that each broad expectation has specific parts to it. Children under seven need to see these specifics visually in order to understand them, so showing them pictures of good choices is a great idea.

Being Nice = being nice with your body, your words, and your actions.
Being Helpful = helping your family and friends, your home, and yourself (by doing your best).
Being In Control = controlling your body and actions, your words, and your emotions.

Finally, be on the lookout for good choices. Tell them you noticed when they made a good choice and reinforce the behavior with your attention to it. For example, "I noticed how you were in control of your body when we waited in line at the store. You probably wanted to touch the candy bars but you didn't and that was a good choice."

Let Children Know What Is Not Allowed
"Zero in" on zero tolerance behaviors like:
No Fussing.
No Fighting.
No Hurting.
No Whining.
No Lying.

Choose a few items from this list or your own ideas that make sense in your home. These should be broad enough to cover a lot of ground. Again, visually showing children under age seven examples of these negative behaviors is a good idea so that we can help them better understand what we are talking about. For example:
No Fussing = no whining, no screaming, and no wailing.

Give Your Child Tools to Help Them Regulate Behavior

Give them a chance to rewind and do it over again without the bad choices. Parents may have to give children examples of how they could have done things differently like, "Say that again in a nice way," "Show me how to play nice with your sister," or "Say nothing instead of saying something nasty."

Allow them a chance to take a break. When they are unable to rewind on the spot and give you an alternative to the bad choice, allow them a chance to take a break away from the group and return on their own when they are ready to be nice. This break is not a negative consequence but just a chance to regroup. They may take it a multitude of different ways and whatever works to get them to regroup is an okay choice for a break. The goal is the regrouping, not the actual break. So help your child decide what is going to work and use it.

Remind them that *nice gets nice and nasty gets nothing.*

Come up with a list of the things that are important to your child and take these things away for a designated period of time if they do not get their behavior on track after rewinding or taking a break. These items can be TV, computers, favorite toys, snacks, or dessert for the day. Make sure what you take away is something meaningful, so that they weigh the consequences of their actions. If you tell them they will lose something, then you *have* to be willing to follow through.

If we set them up with these boundaries and tools, the child should begin to regulate their behavior without us doing it for them. Having rules and systems for how they work will give the child the boundaries and expectations they need to feel secure and safe. Having tools and a system for how they work will give the child the chance to be in charge of their behavior.

The child gets the chance to succeed on his own!

The child gets the chance to stay and play.

The child gets the chance to have special things later in his day.

Thumbs up to parents who use rules and boundaries to help their child bloom and grow!

ACTION STEP: Ask your child to help you design the rules for a certain part of the day. Sometimes their rules, boundaries, and consequences will be more in-depth than the parents'. If your children help you make them, you might get them to follow the rules a little more carefully.

IT'S GONNA GET WORSE!

Things always get worse before they get better. It's a shock to their system for kids to see that parents are on the same page and that the rules and consequences are going to be real and followed through on.

It's already rough, or you probably wouldn't have picked up this book. Now if you begin to implement some of these methods, you might see it gets rougher. **How will you calm the seas of your family life?**

When parents ask me to step in as they try to make a change in their child's behavior, I often say that things will probably get worse before they get better. In other words, you might see your child's behavior escalate as they try to wriggle out of your new set of boundaries. Your child may test you to your last drop of energy so that they can ensure you really mean what you say. But stick with it. Wait them out with the patience of Job and the calm of Jesus walking on water. Rely on prayer partners in the saints who've been through tough times to help you regulate and be at peace through the discord.

When you are trying to make a change in your child's behavior, your days can be dark and dismal, and it can be difficult to find the light at the end of the tunnel. You might wonder if these horribly explosive behaviors will follow your child into their teenage years and end up wrecking your family. These frustrations may make you want to quit before you even begin to make a difference, but I say hang on and zone into the smallest moments of growth.

It is essential in the midst of this kind of turmoil for parents to identify the smallest pinprick of light or growth when they see it in their child's behavior.

If all day they have tested you, but for one short second, you witness an act of kindness, you have to nab the moment and call it like you see it. "I noticed when I asked you to get your coat on, you listened on the first time," "I noticed you allowed your little brother to sit beside you while you played with your trains," "I noticed that earlier today, you didn't cry when it was time to leave the park." In the midst of a crazy day it can be so easy to overlook these small moments of success because they are outnumbered by bad choices and because frankly, the bad choices are usually noisier and more apt to catch your attention.

So force yourself to be on the lookout for these shining moments (even if they seem to be the smallest deed or action). I believe that the more you see and recognize their good choices, the more these positive behaviors will repeat themselves.

Eventually you might have trouble finding a bad choice in your child's day because the good choices will shine so brightly. Wouldn't that be a wonderful problem to have?

ACTION STEP: Find pinpricks of hope. Write them down so you find hope in the shifts that are happening, even if they are oh so subtle. Getting through the first change is honestly the hardest and what I have found is that the next layers of change happen more readily because the child sees that you really were able to follow through and now they know you mean business. Write down the pinpricks of hope. Lean on the following saints to inspire you to hang in there: St. John Paul II "I plead with you—never, ever give up on hope; never doubt, never tire and never become discouraged," St. Catherine of Siena "Nothing great is ever achieved without enduring much," and St. Padre Pio of Pietrelcina. They understood that the suffering will bring great things.

I SAY, PLAY!

There is no time like the present to put yourself all into having fun with your kids. Play helps create the positive relational connections that ease the path of adding in discipline and boundaries later.

Plan a weekly game night. Book it on your calendar. Then turn off the TV and video games, put away your phone or iPad, and leave the dirty dishes in the sink. Meet your family at the kitchen table or some cozy spot around your house and play an old favorite.

Even your littlest ones can join in on a more advanced game if you choose a game where they can have a job to do or a modified version made just for them. Allow yourself to bend the rules, and make the game fit your family's style, time frame, and specific needs and interests. Let the kids get creative and allow them to add new rules to the game. This can mean simply tweaking the smallest procedure or objective so that you can play it with a new spin and the kids get to feel like they are in charge of the fun.

If you meet weekly for your family game night, allow a different family member to pick the game for next week. Add it to the calendar so it is planned in stone. If you're consistent, your kids won't worry that they haven't had a chance to choose the game because they will know their turn is right around the corner.

While you play together, keep your eyes open so that you can see new skills you didn't know your child had. Maybe that third grader is an aspiring banker, or maybe your preschooler has fine motor skills that help him succeed at building great traps in the game *Mousetrap*. Let them see you relax and focus on them while you smile and engage in the fun.

While you play, observe their behavior. Catch them when they are acting respectfully or when they have followed directions. Be specific and note exactly what you see that is positive. For example, "Kerry, I noticed you asked your brother if you could help him move his game piece when it was out of his reach," or "Tim, when you found out that Mark was the winner of the game I noticed that you were upset but you didn't yell or scream. You just said, 'Good game.'" Tell them you noticed their good sportsmanship and polite behavior, and then watch them try to repeat the positive behavior over and over again.

When it comes to winning or losing, allow them to suffer through the losses naturally so that they learn it is a part of life. Set boundaries from the beginning for sportsmanship and consequences for the inevitable fussing, hurting, or quitting. Write these boundaries, rules, or consequences on paper or draw a picture to depict what will happen when kids don't make good choices. When and if those negative behaviors come up, simply point and state, "The rules say, 'No fussing or you will lose a point.'"

Soon enough your schedule will be booked with homework, parent teacher conferences, and holiday plans, so make a date weekly to connect on a positive level with your children. Use these moments with your children as "parentable moments" where you show your child how to play nicely and let them see that your family knows how to relax and have fun together. **Make it a Game Night tonight.**

ACTION STEP: It doesn't have to be a board game. What about a game of freeze tag or capture the flag in the backyard? What about making up a new game with the gigantic blow-up ball your kindergartener got for his birthday? The only rules are family and fun.

CUTE DOESN'T CUT IT

Our job as parents is to go beyond the surface with our kids. Making sure we do the heart and head work means caring about what matters most.

Believe me, I am the first to melt when I see a little girl with ruffles on her dress or an adorable young preschooler with a Cincinnati Reds jersey to match his MLB hat. I simply love to find a good deal on great clothes for kids, and my own children know that when it comes to a photo op, cute clothes matter to their mom. I don't have to tell you how expensive it can be to ensure your kid is the cutest kid to walk into the classroom. The children's clothing market is hot. There are options all over the web for parents to find great outfits for great prices, and then shower their kids with designer labels.

The other day I was at a restaurant and saw the most darling curly-haired child dressed in the sharpest duds. His seersucker shorts and designer green polo shirt were so sweet. His shoes may have cost more than my weekly grocery bill, and his monogrammed belt was one of a kind. Mom and Dad had obviously spent time, money, and energy addressing this little guy's style. There is no doubt about it. He was adorable, but his poor choices and out of control behavior were all I could see. If only his demeanor were as enchanting as his appearance. He was spitting his food out, yelling "YUCK!", and "I hate this!" He was running around the dining area screaming with glee as Mom and Dad sipped wine and smiled at him. "Isn't he so cute?"

I say simply, cute doesn't cut it!

I would love to see a world where parents invest in resources that support positive behavior. It's time for parents to spend less time surfing the web for great deals on ribbons and bows and more time finding ideas on how to get their child to pay attention to the rules of their home. I would like to see more Facebook posts where parents recognize and share their child's good choices instead of their adorable Easter Bunny photo shoot.

Dig deep into your parenting approaches and decide what matters most to you and your spouse. Then set up house rules that mirror what you expect. Instead of focusing on how great your child looks in the mirror, make sure their behavior mirrors your family expectations. Are they a friend to the neighbor kids? Are they accepting of people who are different from them? Do they help around the house and wait patiently for their turn to talk or play? Can you take them to a restaurant without getting dirty looks from other customers?

How cute would everyone's children be if they could all sit quietly and attend to a task, use kind words, share their things, and listen on the first time.

It is easy to get caught up in cute. The world around us is telling parents that being cute is the most important thing, but parents of a **Child in Bloom** know the difference. Cute only goes so far, and when parents and their children bloom, the sky's the limit.

One place where cute doesn't cut it is the night out at a restaurant. Others simply think your little one, all dolled up in their cute attire screaming and running around the joint, has got to get it together so that they can enjoy their night out. So be aware that you will need to bring your rules and boundaries on the road and to the restaurant too.

ACTION STEP: See these quick tips for dining with your little ones.

1. Set up a visual storyline before going to the restaurant that tells your child what to expect, how we behave politely, and what the consequences will be if rules are not followed.

2. Practice these same rules at your own dinner table and when playing pretend restaurant with your child at home. Practice and remind your child of these expectations over and over again.

3. Follow through the first time if your child doesn't follow the plan.
4. Find ways to make dining developmentally appropriate. Your child's attention matches directly to their age so bring more than enough stuff to keep them entertained.
5. Ask for a table that is remote and far away from diners who want to have a quiet evening away.
6. Booths are always a good choice for spreading out and giving your child the room they need to wiggle and giggle.
7. Order your child's food in advance and let your waiter know you might need to leave in a hurry when the child has lost their steam.
8. Bring food and drinks to offer while you wait.
9. Have an exit plan that involves getting up to peek at the restaurant's fish tank or walk to the parking lot to get a breather. Never let your child roam a restaurant freely.
10. Pay attention to your child and put your phones to the side as you focus on this special time with your family.
11. When dining with older kids, leave the phones in the car, under their chairs, or in someone's purse. We've all seen a family where all members are glued to their phones throughout dinner. Tech and phones have no place at the dinner table.

SIBLING SAVVY

Acknowledge openly the mixed emotions of having and being a sibling.

Here is the honest truth: It is clear to me that brothers and sisters don't always get along. We have a choice to make as their parents and what we decide could make or break the rest of our time together. Here are three responses that parents make when dealing with the brothers and sisters living in their home:

1. The Positive Parent

We can insist on positive relations between our children at all times. Saying things like "You are brothers and you will be best friends for a lifetime no matter what" or "You are lucky to have a sister, so hug and make up." Or when we hear things like, "I don't like you!" or "You make me so mad!" we could quickly cut the conversation off and make them feel ashamed for being negative with their words and emotions. When we choose this approach, it may seem like we are helping our kids solidify positive relations with each other. For the short term it might silence the negative emotions, but what we might be doing in the long term is creating more resentment because the honest negative emotions are not allowed to surface. Somebody in the situation might feel like they have to go along and say nothing so as not to risk the family peace.

2. The Negative Parent

We could settle into a doom and gloom perspective when our children start to fight, assuming the worst—that they will never get along. We might say things like, "My oldest and youngest just can't get along, I know their personalities just don't mesh and never will" or "All my kids do is bicker. They will never get along so why bother making them be friendly with each other now?" When we choose this perspective, we emphasize their differences, encourage the negative relationship, and avoid honest conversation about how to get beyond the differences. It can become a situation where we portray them as enemies and they repeat the behavior over and over again, assuming it is their role in the family. Once that portrayal happens, it becomes almost like an expectation or script within the family. The child stays in character and the mindsets become fixed.

3. The Balanced Child in Bloom Parent

Here is a third solution for dealing with sibling emotions. What if we acknowledge the mixed emotions and have our children tell us the truth of how they feel? Even if the truth hurts ("I can't stand to be around my baby sister," "I don't want him to be my brother anymore," "I hate her," "I wish he would go away") we can at least allow them to get the emotions off their chest. We can begin by saying things to them that reinforce the truth of what they are feeling, "I understand that sometimes you wish you had Mom and Dad all to yourself" or "I get what you are saying, you are annoyed by your little sister today."

Once they share the emotion, they may begin to problem solve on their own about how to get along. If they can't tell you how they really feel out loud, then have them express it in another way. They can do this through writing, drawing, using puppets, storytelling, or acting it out. Then start to focus on the positives, even the smallest moments when your children *are* getting along. Allow them to recognize these moments. Then help them to realize that even though the truth is that they don't always get along, they do have moments when they *can* connect. These positive moments may begin to happen more often as the children find things they have in common and when we acknowledge the mixed emotions of being siblings.

ACTION STEP: Try to say something different today than what you would have said yesterday. If you tend to lean into the Positive Parent approach to sibling rivalry, try on the Negative Parent approach and eventually you might land right in the middle at a balanced approach.

SAME AND DIFFERENT

Pause and take a moment to ensure every kid is seen and heard. Foster positive times that lead to deep bonds that stand the test of time.

If you were to meet my sister or brother you would know right away that we were related. You would see the family resemblance in our eyes and our expressions. You would listen and laugh along with us as we shared crazy stories from our childhood. We have many things in common: our mannerisms, our experiences, our family, friends, and all the unique stories from our life together. The longer you spend time with us the clearer it would become to you that we are also very different. Our interests, talents, and needs are specific to each one of us, yet we had to live under the same roof, have the same parents, and share everything else in our home. It is a paradox that children who are siblings can be so alike in their experiences and yet so different. This paradox seems to be the root of what causes sibling rivalry and the mixed emotions of having a sister or brother.

Here are two things to keep in mind when raising sisters and brothers:

1. Your children will not be alike in all things, so your parenting approaches will need to be unique to them. Each child will have their own desires, affinities, and needs and it is very likely that they will be different from your own. It is your role as parent to foster these things in your child, so that their true selves can come alive. When we let our children "shine" individually, we will be less likely to compare them and more likely to show them a love that is equal despite their differences.

2. Because they live together under one roof and share life experiences, your children will also have a unique bond that cannot be replicated. These shared experiences will lead to a common language, based upon similar experiences within your home and family life. Hopefully these bonds will be the thread that ties them together despite their differences. They will be connected by their inside jokes and funny family stories that retell their shared experiences. If we as parents make these connections positive and foster special connections, we can help them hold their relationships together. Help your children foster these unique relationships by fostering positive responses to each other. Have open conversations about the mixed emotions of sisterhood and brotherhood. Celebrate both their differences and their common ground. Foster this as a trusting space where every child feels heard and seen.

ACTION STEP: Use a good old-fashioned Venn diagram to plot out how your kids are unique and the same, then remind them that they have those things in common. Put value on the differences that enrich your family life. And don't be too worried if those positive relationships overshadow their love for you. You want your kiddos to gang up on you, make fun of you, and have their inside jokes about you and your spouse. It means they know how to team up. When you are old and gray and heading to a nursing home, you will be glad that they can team up to take care of you!

SAFE SORRY'S

Help kids step out on a limb and say they are sorry in creative ways.

Even as adults it can be difficult to say those three little words—"I am sorry."

When it comes to siblings who have a built-in competitive nature, it can be downright impossible to form those words on their lips. Even when Mom and Dad threaten to take dessert away for weeks, the child in question can hold on without apology and overlook the promise of an ice cream sundae after dinner in an effort to save face. He knows what he did was wrong, he just can't give his sister the pleasure of knowing he made a bad choice. It becomes a control situation, and no matter what, he will not budge.

When this happens, parents can give their child a fresh perspective. **By making a list of the options they have in terms of apologizing, we can give them the control they desire and options that will make them feel safe as they step out on a limb and admit they made a mistake.**

Together with your family take some time during the day (when everything is peaceful around your home) and make a list of all the different ways you can say you're sorry. Chime in with ways you have said you are sorry through actions or other words in your own life. Let them know that it can be hard for adults to say sorry, too, but it is something that has to be done. Let them come up with creative ways to say they are sorry to friends or siblings. When the time comes, and we know that time could be anytime soon, especially during the summer months when siblings spend lots of time together, they can refer to the list and choose the way that makes them feel most comfortable.

Here are a few ideas to get your family's list started:

- Shake hands.
- Smile and nod.
- Write a note.
- Give a gift.
- Make up for what you did.
- Pat the person on the back.
- Help their sibling's "boo-boo" feel better.
- Ask what you can do to help them feel better.
- Tell a joke.
- Make a picture.
- Say it in a different way. "I shouldn't have done that," "I wish I could take it back," "I feel bad about what I did," "I did not want to hurt you," "I'm not going to do that again."

The list can go on and on and can be determined based on what feels natural in your family. When you use this list of options regularly it can allow the power struggle to go away and peace to reenter the sibling relationship again. In fact, the next time you or your spouse have to say you're sorry to someone, you might want to steal an idea from the list of options.

ACTION STEP: Make sure your list is set in a place where you can come to it easily. The more you refer to the list, the more natural it will become to use it.

THERE IS NO "I" IN PARENT

To be very honest, your child could care less if he makes you happy. Encourage him to do it for himself.

When you are talking to your child about their behavior, try to avoid the following "I" statements:

- "**I** don't like it when you scream in my face."
- "**I** am going to take away a toy."
- "**I** want you to make a good choice."
- "**I** am going to put you in time-out."

All of these statements put you (the parent) in the driver's seat. You will spend your day regulating their behavior instead of encouraging them to be in control of their choices. We want them to recognize the benefits of their good behavior; the ways that good choices influence their lives for the better. So next time you find yourself in a tug of war with your child, try statements that give the ownership back to them like these:

"When **you** scream in my face, **you** are telling me that **you** are too angry to make a good choice. Take a break and come back when **you** are ready to talk nicely without screaming."

The child should find a spot to cool down and take enough time to get their anger under control. They should return on their own time but only when they are ready to talk nicely without screaming

"When **you** play with your toys too roughly, **you** are telling me that **you** aren't taking care of them and **you** need a break from the toy."

The child will have to take a break from the toy because they did not play nicely with it. The point is they caused it to be taken away and they can also cause it to stay put if they turn their behavior around.

"If **you** make a good choice, **you** can stay at the park. If **you** do not, **you** will have to go home. I bet you can make a good choice that will turn your day around."

The choices they make affect their day. When we act unaffected by their choices then it is the child's problem to turn it around so they can get the positive consequence they desire.

Once we take the "I" out of the discussion with our children, they have to take the behavior on themselves and not wait for us to reprimand and deliver consequences. It becomes their problem to fix, not ours. When we allow them to have the power to change their own behavior, we have helped them to see that they can control their responses and therefore control their day. By taking ourselves out of the equation, it allows us to be less emotional about the choices they make.

Then the only "I" statements you will have to make will be positive reinforcement statements like these:

- "**I** am proud of you."
- "**I** love you."
- "**I** knew you could do it."
- "**I** noticed you turned your day around."
- "**I** caught you making a good choice."
- "**I** like how you are playing nicely with your toys."

ACTION STEP: Obviously all this is easier said than done. Here are some quick steps to better parenting:

1. Start out by paying attention to your responses to your child's behavior.
2. Begin to put them in the driver's seat when it comes to regulating their behavior.
3. Choose positive reinforcing "I" statements that let them know you have faith that they can turn their day around on their own. Give it a try! I know you can do this!

TOOTLES TO TATTLING

If you are so busy tooting your sibling's horn, you won't have time to tattle.

If your house is anything like mine, you have children who spend their days tattling on their siblings and you spend your day refereeing the arguments.

When we acknowledge the tattling, the accusing child gets two bonuses:

First, they reported a negative behavior and "saved the day."

Second, they feel like they have moved up in the ranks of rivalry because their brother or sister will surely move down after being caught red-handed.

Here's a typical tattling scenario:

> The children are playing a game nicely.
>
> All is good in the home. Mom and Dad are smiling. *Aaahh.*
>
> The parent gives no attention to the children because they think, "Why mess with a good thing?"
>
> Suddenly the climate of the play changes.
>
> Something is unfair and the dice get thrown across the game table.
>
> A child yells, "I quit. Mom and Dad, Josh cheated!"
>
> Mom and Dad are forced to pay attention.
>
> Mom and Dad have to weed through the sequence of the showdown.

Mom and Dad have to figure out the consequences of the actions.

Mom and Dad have a headache.

What if the scenario went a different way:

Dad walks by the table where the children are playing nicely and makes a specific comment about something positive he sees them doing. "I noticed that you let your brother go first."

Dad reinforces that they should try to work out their differences as arguments come up and make it fair so everyone can continue the game. "What is your plan if someone thinks something is unfair?"

Dad mentions he wants each brother or sister to catch their siblings doing something good during the game and report back to him when they are finished.

The children's focus will turn from personal gain to group gain. They will be able to report how well the game went, how well they worked together to solve problems, and Mom and Dad no longer have to be the referees.

They will work through problems as they come up with and focus on the positives instead of the negatives. All the while they will be noticing their sibling's strengths.

This is called positive peer reinforcement, and it is something that teachers are trying to do more and more within their class settings. **Some people call this tootling because it causes children to focus on the positive instead of negative behaviors, replacing tattling with "*tooting* some else's horn."** You can try this in the home setting too.

Here are some steps to make it a success:

1. Mom and Dad specifically call out positive behavior when they see it and clearly state the positive behavior they would like to see.

2. Children focus on catching each other making the good choices that match Mom and Dad's plan.

3. Children report the good choices that others made (instead of tattling on the "bad choices").

4. Positive behavior increases as children work to get the positive attention of their siblings and parents.

5. Shift happens from personal gain to group gain.

6. Children team up to be good.

7. Mom and Dad cease being the referees.

8. Everyone is a little more positive and peaceful.

As parents, you might want to tally up the "tootles" at the end of the day and acknowledge the positive choices made. You could even have your children work towards achieving a certain number of tootles for a family surprise.

Studies show that the rate of positive behaviors go up when positive behaviors are emphasized, recognized, and acknowledged. Likewise, negative behaviors increase when we continue to emphasize, recognize, and acknowledge them. So focus on the positive to get a peaceful home.

Toot your child's horn today!

ACTION STEP: There is a science to this. Track tattling for a while before you start this new plan of tootling. Then add in some training on tootling. Begin to track the tattling to see if when the rate of tattling goes down, does the rate of tootling go up? Have your kids track along with you to make the biggest impact on their relationships.

RESOURCE CONNECTION: Read "Increasing tootling: The effects of a peer-monitored group contingency program on students' reports of peers' presocial behaviors" by Christopher H. Skinner.

RULES RULE

Without rules, chaos ensues.

Rules for your city.

Rules for your church.

Rules for your library.

Rules for a classroom.

Rules for a school.

Rules for eating.

Rules for traveling in a car.

Rules for riding a bike.

Rules for. . .

The list of rules in our world could go on and on, but the rule of thumb is that every part of our day runs smoothly when there are expectations set up in advance and when everyone knows what is going on.

What if a library did not set up rules to govern how we borrow and return books? What if once food was on the table there were no rules that labeled how and where you were supposed to eat it? What if when driving in our car we did not clearly know the rules of the road? There could be utter chaos, no one would feel safe, and there would be no order.

The same chaos and mess could end up taking over your home if you do not begin to take a step in the right direction and devise a list of your house rules.

If using the word "rules" bothers you, then simply call them systems, expectations, boundaries, or your house motto.

Start with what you expect. These should be the three basic overarching goals for behavior such as: be nice, be a good listener, and be honest. You should then detail what this does and doesn't look like. Next you should identify a system as to how these rules will be followed and how Mom and Dad's responses will try to increase positive behavior and decrease negative behavior.

Give your child a clear list of zero tolerance behaviors including basic statements that cover a lot of territory. For example, there will be no hurting, fussing, or fighting.

Then give them tools to work through the inevitable mess ups.

1. Allow them to rewind when they feel like they want to retell something in a nicer way, or when they want to redo an action or word that came out of their mouth.
2. Tell them that taking a break and coming back ready to make good choices is what adults do all the time when they say things like, "I will be taking a quick walk and then I will be right back to talk this through." Let them know it is a possible way to help them get their behavior back on track.
3. Discover alternative ways to solve the problem. If you are fighting over homework, allow the child to decide where they will do their homework, inside the play tent in the basement or at their desk in their room.

By giving them tools for success that could help them turn their behavior around, you are giving them a chance to redo the behavior and learn from it. They will begin to repeat the positive behaviors and omit the negative behaviors once they know the systems, consequences, expectations, and rewards of following through on your house rules.

ACTION STEP: Can your kids name the rules around your city? I bet they can. Then see if they can name the unwritten rules around your home. If not, it's time to sit down and note the rules.

BETTER THINGS TO DO... REALLY?

What could be better than growing saints among us?

I was recently next to a parent when I heard them tell their child "I've got better things to do than to help you with your homework all day." The parent and child were at an indoor sporting facility attempting to work through homework while they waited for a sibling to finish their practice. Guess what the better thing to do was? Yep! Checking their Facebook account. This parent voiced what many of us are showing with our responses to our children. What are your responses telling your child? There is no doubt about it, life with kids in tow is busy. Sports, work commitments, schoolwork, home projects, and keeping up with our social lives all add to the hectic pace.

The bad news is many times children play second fiddle to these other commitments and parents lash out saying, "Hurry up, get going, I have got better things to do," as they rush their children from place to place.

The good news is children are resilient and need only the smallest portion of your time. Fifteen minutes playing catch in the backyard, ten minutes reading their favorite book, five minutes connecting with them about their day, one minute consoling them when they are sick, one second to pat them on the back.

When looking at your to-do list, could you add in small moments like this to your hectic day? Or do you have "better things to do"?

What could be better than the most important job?

ACTION STEP: Make a list of the things you inadvertently say are better than parenting, by saying (without saying directly) "I have better things to do."

"ME FIRST" GOES LAST

Teach your child to be a servant leader or humbly take a step back and allow someone else to be in charge.

The following phrases are normal responses from your toddler, preschooler, or maybe even your grade school child.

- "I want to be the boss!"
- "I want the best toy!"
- "I don't like to share!"
- "I get the biggest cookie!"
- *"Me first!"*

Remember that at these developmental stages, your child is literally the center of their own universe. They plan on having their way no matter what.

You, on the other hand, have a different plan. You are hoping that they will turn out to be compassionate, caring, and kind. You shudder when you hear the above responses because you know they don't match this plan.

How do you help your child work through the *"mine, mine, mine!"* mentality so that they can get along with others? How about instilling this house rule? **"Me first" always goes last.**

What does that mean? If you claim it first, you will most certainly have it last. If you grab the biggest piece first, you will most definitely have the smallest piece on your plate later. If you yell "Me first!" as you race to stand in line, you will be heading to the end of the line without a doubt.

This approach will go against your child's natural will to survive. He will not like playing second fiddle to his friend or brother. She will hate being last in line to get a treat. However, if you instill a natural tendency to allow others to step in front of you, I believe you are on your way to helping your child bloom into the gentleman or gentlewoman you have dreamed them to be. Instead of saying "Mine, mine, mine," they may start to say, "What do you need?" "What do you want?" "How can I help?" or "What can I share?"

Imagine a kindergarten class filled with children who step back and let another child take the lead. Imagine a group of teenagers patiently waiting until everyone else is served before grabbing the last piece of pizza. Imagine a world where children and adults instinctively think of their neighbor before they think of themselves. Imagine "Me last!"

ACTION STEP: Share the Litany of Humility with your children and talk about how they can emulate it by visiting https://www.ewtn.com/catholicism/devotions/litany-of-humility-245.

BIBLE VERSE: "But many who are first will be last, and many who are last will be first" (Matthew 19:30).

CHUGGING VS. CRUISING

Determine and understand what the speed of your parenting is.

The following was a favorite rhyme around our house when our two oldest children were still into reading board books. Once it faded, they were onto *Diary of a Wimpy Kid* and other books like that, but the rhyme rings true to me as I think about the rhythm of life with kids in tow.

Train chugs. . . clickety clack.

Engine upfront. . . caboose in back.

Passing cows. . . Moooo!

Over the river. . . Whooo, Whooo!

In the world of parenting, there seems to be two speeds:

1. **Chugging** through the changes wondering if we'll ever get through this terrible stage

or

2. **Cruising** quickly through our days, barely pausing to look around at the wonderful scenery of our lives.

The uphill battle of making a change in our child's behavior response or routine can seem overwhelming as we are right in the middle of it. But the good news is we can get through these changes and wipe our brow as we speed away from the mountain behind us, saying, "Whooo, Whooo!"

To stay on the right track, keep these things in mind:

1. **Know where you are headed.**
   Use your family's vision or goals to design your expectations for the trip. Knowing what you expect and where you want your children to be in terms of behavior helps you to see the value in the extra effort you will put forth during this part of your parenting journey. Seeing the station on the other side of the mountain might just give you the extra boost you need to make it up the hill.

2. **An object in motion stays in motion.**
   As long as we have the energy to get started and we keep it up, ("I think I can, I think I can,") we will stay in motion and eventually make it to the top. This energy means we have to take care of ourselves, we have to dig into all our resources (books, friends, past experiences, and family support) and use them to help us push through to the goal which is well-behaved children. "I know you can!"

3. **Keep positive.**
   On your way up the hill *("clickety clack, clickety clack")* it may feel like you are about to break down, but if you look closely, you will notice the scenery changing. Even the smallest positive step in the right direction should be noted. Tell yourself, "I did it. I kept my cool and didn't show any emotion when I was frustrated with Johnny's behavior." Or tell your child, "Wow, I noticed how you listened on the first time." Catching every single one of these positives will give you and your child a little more momentum to keep chugging.

ACTION STEP: There is no doubt about it, the tough times will keep coming, but they may seem a little less overwhelming when we keep these things in mind.

BIBLE VERSE: "Blessed is the one who perseveres under trial because, having stood the test, that person will receive the crown of life that the Lord has promised to those who love him" (James 1:12).

THE REAL THREE R'S

These are the three things that serve as a base for all parenting.

I could never figure out why educators referred to the three R's (reading, writing, and arithmetic) knowing full well that only one of those words starts with an "R." Why would they use this to help them remember the major components of their field of work, knowing full well they might just confuse the children they are working with and create more spelling headaches for everyone?

I have been referring to my own three R's of teaching for the last few years as I work with future educators at the college level. These teachers will one day go on to run their own classrooms or work as special educators. I know that throughout their career they will have to be lifelong learners who are able to problem solve and create new approaches to deal with each unique issue that enters their room. I want them to have three key components that will consistently help them guide their decision making. They will need to be **RESOURCEFUL**, **REFLECTIVE**, and **RESPONSIBLE** at all times.

These same three components may help parents succeed as well.

1. Be Resourceful: Be a lifelong learner, and continue to connect with great books, websites, and information that can lead you to better understand your child and the developmental levels they are passing through. Be connected to other parents, educators, and support groups that can help you to see that you are not alone in the quest to be a better parent. Use their suggestions to begin your thought processes and planning.

2. Be Reflective: Take what you have gathered from watching your child, reading up on new strategies, and connecting to other parents and educators. Then reflect on your resource's ideas and make them your own. How do the approaches fit your parenting style? What can you tweak to make this approach a better fit for you? Step by step, design a plan for consequences and try to revise what isn't working. Resolve to make it better.

3. Be Responsive: Act on what you know and what you have thought about. Change your responses based upon what your child needs. Try out a new response even if it isn't what you feel comfortable doing at first. Use specific tactics, styles, tones, and multisensory approaches like visuals and songs to guide your responses to your children.

Parents who use these three R's to help them work through problems will succeed.

ACTION STEP: List how you can increase your resourcefulness, reflection, and responsiveness. List concrete ways you make these things more prevalent in your life.

BEDTIME BASICS

Routines matter, especially when everyone is tired at bedtime, including Mom and Dad.

Here are a few of the bedtime ideas I have used in the past. Although they may seem like common knowledge, many parents seem to omit these key items in their bedtime plans.

- **Routines.**
- **Positive interactions.**
- **Support for negative feelings.**
- **Clear boundaries.**

1. Allow the child to have some say in routines.

   Allow them to make choices about how their nighttime routine will go. "Should we brush teeth first or put pajamas on first? Should we leave a hall light on or a nightlight? Should we have one or two stuffed friends in our bed?" Notice all the choices are livable and ones that you can both agree upon. Once you have settled on a plan, set up a visual schedule or checklist that is followed routinely every night and at nap time. Check it off as you go. Your child will feel safe knowing the routine, you will have a boundary to set the tone of the routine, and your child will feel empowered and excited that they were able to choose what makes them feel comfortable.

2. Use these key steps and routine moments to connect with your child via calming interactions.

   Listen to their favorite calming music, recite or read prayers, tell or read a story, have the child tell you a story, recite rhymes or poems, help them to retell their day reinforcing all the "growing" and good things they did that day, or sing songs about each step in your nighttime routine like teeth brushing *(The ABC's)* and getting pajamas on *(It's Pajama Time)*.

3. Connect to the child's emotions and let them know you understand their fears and needs.

"I know you like a light on, which light should I leave on for you tonight?" Or "I know you feel alone, which stuffed animal would you like to join you in bed tonight?"

4. Set clear ending points, consequences, and boundaries and follow through by taking away something they want.

"If you choose to get out of your bed tonight, I will have to take Bear away because he is tired and needs his sleep. Bear can sleep in another room if you cannot make a good choice and fall asleep without fussing." Notice the ownership of the problem becomes the child's to solve, not yours. Hmm? I wonder what they will choose—bear or fussing?

5. If you find yourself and your child in a rut, switch up the routine.

Ask the child to help you form a new plan for bedtime, and then phase them into the new routine. Phasing in and out items is the best option rather than quitting cold turkey. Focus on one thing to phase in or out and work through it for at least three days before changing anything else.

ACTION STEP: What plans do you have in place for bedtime routines? Could your child rattle them off? If not, they might be missing consistency.

ONE SHINING MOMENT

Don't miss your child's one shining moment.
It could be your moment to shine, too.

When we watch basketball in our house, it's time to cheer on our teams to victory. At the end of the season there will be one team that gets the title, wins it all, and has the big moment. The song that they will play to commemorate this season of madness will focus on all the little moments that mean a lot and add up to one great season of basketball.

As a parent, are you so busy looking for the big victory that you overlook the one shining moment that could change the course of your child's day?

Your fourth grader begs you to shoot hoops in the backyard but you say, "I can't. I'm busy designing plays so your little league basketball team can win that big trophy at the end of the season." To your daughter, the "big trophy" might be the smile on her face as she beats you in a game of HORSE.

Your three year old brings you his favorite book to read, but you say, "I can't. I have to check my email one more time in case I closed that big deal." To your three year old the "big deal" might be the story they've waited for all evening.

Your teenager leaves his messy room, climbs up onto the kitchen counter, and tries to engage you in a conversation about something that happened at school today, but you say, "Can I just have a moment to myself? I have to cook for this big event in our neighborhood." To your teenager the "big event" might be the conversation he needs to have with you about the peer pressure he has been feeling at school lately.

Oftentimes we are so focused on the big stuff (trophies, titles, deals, and events) that we overlook the small shining moments. These small moments may lead us into closer communion with our child.

Be present as you walk through your days of parenting so that you don't overlook your time to shine as a beacon of love to your child. It could be your one shining moment.

ACTION STEP: Make a list of your shining moments as a parent. It's okay if not every moment is so shiny!

FROM GHOSTS TO GOALS

Don't be ruled by the Ghosts of Parenting Past or Future.

Do you recall the Staples commercial that is shown during the back to school rush every August? The father is skipping and jumping down the aisles of the store, singing a classic tune, and celebrating that his children will soon be spending the majority of their day at school.

In contrast, around the holidays, the same song is played over and over on the radio, but many parents begin shuttering at the idea that they will have to spend two full weeks with their children over the holiday break. Suddenly, it doesn't feel like "the most wonderful time of the year."

As you look toward this extra time with your children, do you squeal with glee like Tiny Tim on Christmas morning, or do you hunch over and roll your eyes like Ebenezer Scrooge and say, "Bah humbug"?

There is some good news for parents in *The Christmas Carol* that Dickens penned so many years ago. Even Scrooge changed his perspective. What would happen if you took a stroll with a few of your old friends, the Ghost of Parenting Past and the Ghost of Parenting Future, and used them to help guide you to a better place of parenting with purpose?

A visit from the Ghost of Christmas Past brings Scrooge to witness all that happened prior to the present moments of his life and all that influenced his bad mood today. What Ghost of Parenting Past do you allow to creep into your day? Do you hang onto the old negative parenting styles passed on through the generations of your family? Do you replay parenting mistakes you made yesterday and feel unsure how to move forward from them today? When we spend our present parenting moments hanging onto these ghosts from our past, do we leave any room in our hearts to focus on our child today?

Maybe for you it is the Ghost of Parenting Future that clouds your present moments with your children. These ghosts can keep you up at night as the "what ifs," "maybes," and "oh no's" consume your every thought. These anxious thoughts of what your child's future holds take up room in your heart that could be spent instead on celebrating the great things happening today.

In the end, Scrooge moved beyond these ghosts and headed into Bob Cratchit's family celebration. He finally saw Christmas for what it truly is—a precious time of joy and pleasure.

I believe that childhood should be described in the same way. **Parents that bloom release themselves from the trappings of past and future and simply focus on today. When they do this, they can change their family experiences and help their child bloom and grow!**

The smile on your child's face and the warmth in your heart will tell you that you've just given the best present during this "most wonderful time of the year." That present is *you!*

Positive parenting can help you turn your ghosts into goals and give you the tools to change what happens today.

ACTION STEP: Here's a simple list of things to reflect on:

- Focus on the smallest moments within your child's day. Remember moments matter. You don't have to do it all. Even the smallest connection or move in their direction could save the whole day.
- Pay attention to the slightest facial expression, word, and emotion that you share while in your child's presence. They are watching and learning and these modeling moments matter the most.
- Allow today to be alone in its glory, without worrying about what happened yesterday or what might happen tomorrow.

EVERYDAY EPIPHANIES

We pass down all kinds of things to our kids and sometimes these things stick.

Great Grandma Mattson used to say, "Making your bed each day can make your day in every way." This saying probably came from her mother, Great Great Grandmother Mansfield in Terre Haute, Indiana. Like many bits of knowledge, it was passed down through generations. When my kids were tall enough to contribute to the bed-making, my husband and I shared this with our own kids, but they didn't seem to pay much attention—until our fifteen-year-old daughter, Evy, had her own revelation.

One day, she excitedly told me, "Mom, I don't know what it is, but I feel so much better all day when I make my bed." She felt like she had discovered something brand new, even though this advice was old news to me and the generations of people before her. Evy had recently redecorated her room, choosing colors, painting her old bed, and finding accessories to match. Her room was like something straight out of HGTV and it was all her doing. So it shouldn't have surprised me that she was now embracing the advice I had given but claiming it as her own.

She felt a sense of ownership over her newly designed room and wanted to take good care of it. Of course, my own pride wanted to speak up and say, "I told you so," but instead, I played along as if her insight was a new revelation to me too. But my epiphany was something more than hers. It was at this moment when I realized things were changing between us. With only three years left under our roof, it was becoming her life to lead and her bed to make, not mine. She was separating from me but the interesting thing that happened within that separation was a kind of new and eternal bond. **The kind of bond that comes with wisdom and passing through the generations.**

She could find the latest life hacks or trendy tips from social media and feel like she found the golden ticket to happiness. She had these kinds of knowledge nuggets before, but what she had now was a little bit of wisdom, the kind that comes from personal experience and changes us into something new and different.

I too was gaining wisdom and had been since I was her age. The wisdom gained in this tiny moment was about knowing when to guide her and when to let her learn on their own. The wisdom became an epiphany for me when I realized this as a positive next step, not a heartbreaking loss. She didn't need me as much as she once did. She was learning on her own and taking ownership of her things and growing up and becoming separate from me in concrete ways and connecting back to me in ways that would be generational, everlasting, and eternal. She was passing on the wisdom of the ages to the next generation and carrying her loved ones that came before her along with her. This is the bittersweet core of parenting. To watch them grow and then grow apart from us knowing that the bonds made will tie you together in unseen ways beyond their childhood.

ACTION STEP: What if next time you feel like saying, "I told you so," you don't?

BIBLE VERSE: "They are not meant to remain as children but to change and grow" (Ephesians 4:14-19).

"HOME TRAINING"

Vow to spend time being home with your kids during their growing years.

My mom and dad moved to a small town in Ohio in 1969 to raise their family. When my dad was choosing a town to settle in, he chose Lancaster, Ohio. On their visit to the city, he had counted the churches and he knew the more churches, the more solid the network of good people to support his business and his family's life.

Just recently one of my mother's best friends sat with me, recalling the storybook childhoods her sons and my siblings and I shared as neighbors while growing up on good old Graham Drive. She said, "We seventies parents didn't have all the books or websites to guide us but we had each other as a network of support and we vowed as moms to home train our kids." I asked her if home training was a certain parenting approach from the seventies. She said it was simply a vow to spend time with our children in our homes during their growing years.

It meant training them within the home setting so that they would take those skills and traits out into the community and spread God's good things. She said no moms on that street worked at the time, but even so, they counted their mothering as the most important job a woman could have. To them it was God's work and His voice calling them to help their children's lives on their path to Glory. In fact, she called it, "Raising kids in the Glory Days," when life was simpler. KNOX Blocks gelatin squares and Tupperware were king and our birthday parties were a simple cake from a box and Kool-Aid from a pitcher. Moms didn't have to strive to do it all and do it all perfectly because they knew who their support networks were—the other women down the street making their way through motherhood.

The goal of home training was to raise kids who cared, were conscientious, independent, and connected in their home life, school life, and social life. We were all well-rounded kids who respected our elders and were confident in our abilities, but never overconfident, just enough to remain humble and be filled with good times and laughter. No matter what their creed, these faith-filled moms on that small town street held tight to their vows and each other as they worked to make it clear that having a good and present parent is the most important job on the planet.

ACTION STEP: Who's in your home training network? How can you come up with more time with your kids so you can be their biggest influencer and prepare them to step into the world ready for what it will bring them?

THE GREAT RESET

Every once in a while, you will need to reel them in.

A friend of ours is a baseball coach and an eighth-grade math teacher. He was coaching our son's team one day, and his tone seemed off. It was abrupt because usually he was jovial. He was pointing in the kids' faces instead of offering encouragement, and when the kids started goofing off on the bench, he walked right into the dugout and firmly said, "No!" He didn't have to yell or scream. He was crystal clear. He was in charge, and the boys immediately straightened up. Silence took over, and they fell in line with the standard rules they had learned on day one but weren't following anymore. They'd been on his team for years, so they knew the routine—listen the first time, sit still, cheer for your friends, do as you're told on the bases, and we'll all get along. They had been doing well, but just lately we could tell that they were pushing the boundaries, that is until the coach sensed they needed a firm reset.

We asked the coach about it later, and he said it was intentional. He used the same approach in his classroom and at home. He explained that kids learn the rules, follow them for a while, and then start to test the boundaries. **When things get out of line, adults need to reinforce the rules and hold the line.** He called it "The Great Reset." It was a way to re-establish the hierarchy, remind them who was in charge, and reboot the system so everyone could get back to having fun, playing, and learning together.

This resonated with us. We had two of our kiddos in high school at the time, and they were starting to do what high schoolers do best—test the boundaries. My husband and I decided to try this approach. When they were being disrespectful or entitled, we would simply say no when it was a time when they assumed we'd simply say yes. We had been busier than normal lately and they were getting by without a lot of questions from us simply because we weren't taking the time to pause and pay attention. But we dropped that "no" in, and it gave us a chance to pause the system and to reset expectations, reminding them how we do and do not act in our home. It also prompted us to reevaluate our rules and ensure we weren't taking anything for granted.

Of course, no child likes to be told no, but sometimes these boundary resets are necessary to maintain a healthy balance. I had done this in my classroom and home life before but it usually came at a hectic time when I was angry and at my wit's end. These well-placed no's we randomly dropped in were done with intention to reset, not as a reaction to stress or disrespect. They were done at a random time to surprise the kids and help them to realize that it's okay not to get everything they want and that sometimes parents say no.

ACTION STEP: Where could you insert a well-placed no, simply to remind your children of your role as a loving authority figure? This isn't a punishment, but rather a way to balance the independence you're fostering in them. It helps them remember the connection between your guidance and the healthy habits and relationships you're helping them build. Ultimately, our goal as parents is to raise children who can thrive independently. This mirrors God's plan for us, to guide us with boundaries out of love so we learn to rely on Him. As we model good teaching, we can reset the rules when needed, just as God does.

BIBLE VERSE: "From one man he made all the nations, that they should inhabit the whole earth; and he marked out their appointed times in history and the boundaries of their lands" (Acts 17:26).

DON'T CLOUD THE COMPLIMENT WITH YOUR BIG "BUT"

Your kids will hear nothing you said before the big "but," so leave it for later.

Our son Peter is a great kid. His teachers and coaches love him, and he's a leader among his friends. Recently, I told my husband how Pete made a great choice that showed maturity. We agreed we should tell him how proud we are. As my husband planned what to say, he made the classic parenting mistake of adding one of those big "buts."

"You're so mature, *but* you haven't practiced tennis all summer."

"You're so smart, your grades are amazing, *but* I wish you'd make your bed."

"Your loyalty to your friends is admirable, *but* I don't like how you treated your sister at the dinner table."

I am not saying that helping our kids get better through encouraging them to practice more, keep their things orderly, and treat their siblings well is not important. I am simply saying that right here in this moment they just need you to be positive. And that simply means to pause with the rest of the line. It can wait for another time. **Pause and be positive if you want those positive behaviors to bloom and grow.** Adding in the "but" can make the powerful compliment wilt away. Those big "buts" can overshadow the compliment to the point that the child doesn't hear anything before them.

ACTION STEP: Next time, slice your sentence off before the big "but." Save it for another talk when you're trying to teach a lesson. For now, leave it alone after the compliment and get your big "but" out of the way. In parenting and life, there is a time for everything. A time to reap the harvest of blooms coming forth from your child's life, and a time to weed out the things they need to change. Compartmentalize these two so your words and feelings around their growth are clear, and they don't get clouded or confused with expecting perfection.

BIBLE VERSE: "There is an appointed time for everything, and a time for every affair under the heavens" (Ecclesiastes 3:1).

SLOW, PAUSE, FEEL, LISTEN, KNOW, AND GO WITH THE NEXT STEP.

If you're too busy to pause, you are too busy.

I've always kept myself busy. I mean like crazy busy, wearing a multitude of hats and trying to get it all done and more. I am not sure why, but perhaps in some ways it is to avoid being overwhelmed by the emotions that would pour out of me if I took the time to feel every bit of emotion that comes with parenting and comes with watching them slowly inch their way out my door.

But now, with more time to pause and less birdies in the nest, I find myself grappling with those very real feelings and the pure nature of time that is fleeting before me. When your kids are young and busy rushing off to the next event or when you are busy balancing it with your own work and accomplishments, it is easy to get caught up in the whirlwind of activities and let the pause pass by. I am here (almost on the other side) begging you to feel the feels, pause and pinch yourself. It's happening, you are raising your family, and they will soon no longer live under your roof.

Take it in and soak it up and don't be so busy that you avoid the reality of all of this. Like a harvester in a field, parenting can feel like hard and busy work. Yet God asks us to see the beauty in the harvest even while we are busy plucking it from the field. This requires us to stop and take it all in. In the slowness and silence that comes with pausing, we may confront difficult emotions, but it's also where we can hear God's voice guiding us and know He has us through all of the changes and can guide us towards the very next step.

Abraham Lincoln told a story about how he used to have to walk blindly to the barn each night and he didn't know how to get there except for the light he carried in his lantern. Even in the pitch dark he made it to the end of the walk to his destination, walking slowing, and that was the key—pausing as needed and relying on God to shed light little by little along the way. This is what happens when we go slow, pause, and take it in little by little while listening and knowing God's guidance. We reach a place that seemed impossible and hard to imagine, but it arrives and because we were awake and aware and feeling along the way, it is easier to take in the changes that arrive with it.

So slow down and pause more. Feel the feels. Listen and know God's guidance. You won't erase all your worries, but you'll find the strength to take the next step, and the next. And when you pause again, you'll see that you've created a masterpiece: raising a child of God.

ACTION STEP: Carve out consistent and intentional moments of pause. Maybe it's in the car as you wait for the kids to pile in or maybe while you take a moment to stare out at them playing in the backyard. Slow down, pause to see what's happening right in front of you, allow the feelings to come, and then listen for God and know that He can and will tell you what to do next. Teach your children to do the same. Slow, pause, feel, listen, know, and go with the next step.

Part Six

Closing It Up

PACK FOR PARENTING

The days are long but the time goes so fast—enjoy the ride!

Like many families, we anxiously await a summer getaway that we planned months ago. The plan includes an ending spot where we will park our family for a few days and savor the sun and relaxation that a vacation brings. I would like you to think about your child's behavior like you might plan a trip.

When you detail your parenting journey, make sure it includes the following:

Choose a destination.

What do you expect to have from your children down the road? How will they be when they leave your nest and enter the real world? What kind of college roommate, coworker, boss, husband, or wife will they become because of your guidance?

Your goals for your child may be that they will be compassionate, kind, gentle, and slow to compete with those around them. Or maybe it is the opposite, and you hope they will be competitive and have a winning attitude. Maybe you would like them to be cautious, calm, and quietly reflective, or maybe that they will be creative and open-minded. Whatever your dream for your child's future, consider it your destination on the parenting journey and know that, like your summer vacation, it will not happen if you don't first set it in motion.

Pack your bags.

Research what you will need. Rely on your resources to fill your bags with tools and tricks that work for your child's developmental stage and temperament. Connect with great parenting resources (people, books, programs, and websites) and bring them along on your journey.

Bring a map.

Put your plan to paper and map out alternative routes to the same destination. Plan ahead for bumpy roads. Know that you might have to use visuals to support your plan. Don't spend all your time in the fast lane, racing from place to place. At times, take the road less traveled (your parenting style doesn't have to be popular).

Round up your passengers.

Who is a part of your plan? What caregivers need to be aware of the plan, besides you? Take every passenger's perspective into consideration (including both parents, caregivers, and grandparents) when you plan so everyone feels like they've been heard and all needs and strengths have been met.

Find rest stops along the way.

Give yourself and your family time to pause, reflect, and regroup as you think about your plan and take care of your passengers.

Get lost.

On the way, it is okay to get lost or stray from the beaten path. At times you will have to be flexible in your thinking because all your passengers may have different needs that don't match up to your plan. To get back on track, you might have to try new perspectives, new ideas, and new approaches.

Remember the parenting journey may not always be comfortable but if you keep plugging along, you will arrive at your destination.

IT'S YOUR DAY—PARENT WITH PAUSE

Pause into your days as a parent and celebrate the growth and understanding that is happening under your roof.

It's your day!

Celebrate. . . Acknowledge. . . Forgive. . . Remember.

Celebrate the fact that you don't have to be perfect at parenting.

Celebrate by finding your own inner kid.

Laugh, leap, and learn with your children!

Acknowledge the sacrifices you have made to make your child's life more complete.

Acknowledge the smallest things you do daily to make your family complete.

Forgive yourself for the mistakes of last week.

Forgive yourself for overlooking that one thing on yesterday's to-do list.

Remember that you have support all around you waiting to give you a lift when you need it most.

Remember that you are not alone!

Remember that these crazy days soon will pass.

As parents together in this most important job
of parenting let's

Celebrate! Acknowledge! Forgive! Remember!

Laugh! Leap! Learn and Love!

It's your day!

MENTIONED RESOURCE CONNECTIONS

Books

The Educator's Guide to Preventing and Solving Discipline Problems by Mark Boynton and Christine Boynton

Your Child's Growing Mind: Brain Development and Learning from Birth to Adolescence by Jane M. Healy, PhD

The Happiest Toddler on the Block: How to Eliminate Tantrums and Raise a Patient, Respectful and Cooperative One- to Four-Year-Old by Harvey Karp, MD

Ages and Stages: A Parent's Guide to Normal Childhood Development by Charles E. Schaefer, PhD and Theresa Foy DiGeronimo

Between: A Guide for Parents of Eight to Thirteen-Year-Olds by Sarah Ockwell-Smith

The Teenage Brain: A Neuroscientist's Survival Guide to Raising Adolescents and Young Adults by Frances E. Jensen, MD and Amy Ellis Nutt

The Spiritual Child: The New Science on Parenting for Health and Lifelong Thriving by Lisa Miller, PhD

The Available Parent: Expert Advice for Raising Successful and Resilient Teens and Tweens by John Duffy, PhD

From Defiance to Cooperation: Real Solutions for Transforming the Angry, Defiant, Discouraged Child by John F. Taylor, PhD

Building Resilience in Children and Teens: Giving Kids Roots and Wings by Kenneth R. Ginsburg, MD

Why Do They Act That Way? A Survival Guide to the Adolescent Brain for You and Your Teen by David Walsh, PhD

Positive Discipline for Teenagers: Empowering Your Teen and Yourself Through Kind and Firm Parenting by Jane Nelsen, EdD and Lynn Lott, MA

Get Out of My Life, But First Could You Drive Me and Cheryl to the Mall? by Anthony E. Wolf, PhD

Parenting with Love & Logic: Teaching Children Responsibility by Foster Cline, MD and Jim Fay

The Soul of Discipline by Kim John Payne, MEd

Articles

Skinner, Christopher H., Tammy H. Cashwell, and Amy L. Skinner. " Increasing Tootling: The Effects of a Peer-Monitored Group Contingency Program on Students' Reports of Peers' Prosocial Behaviors." *Psychology in the Schools 37*, no. 3 (May 2000): 263–70. https://doi.org/10.1002/(sici)1520-6807(200005)37:3<263::aid-pits6>3.0.co;2-c.

Podcasts

Because I Said So! by John Rosemond

Online Resources

"Free Resources." SensationalBrain. https://sensationalbrain.com/free-resources/.

"The Two-Minute Relationship Builder." ASCD. ://ascd.org/el/articles/the-two-minute-relationship-builder.

Renee Mattson, Ph.D. is a former clinical professor of special education at Miami University and Xavier University in Ohio and currently is the coordinator of the Ohio Partnership for Excellence in Paraprofessional Preparation, a statewide grant-funded project supporting inclusive school settings.

A graduate of Xavier University and the University of Cincinnati, her research focus is on collaboration skills for special educators as they share best practices with the paraprofessionals and parents that love and support children with specific needs.

She is the founder of Child in Bloom Parent and Educational Coaching and has supported more than a thousand families across the country helping them gain skills to support parenting their child through the growing years. She also has coached in hundreds of educational settings preparing new and veteran educators to support the children who enter their classrooms with positive, responsive, and differentiated approaches so all kids can fully participate.

Dr. Mattson gives presentational addresses at conferences, training workshops, and retreats for parents and educators. Renee and her best friend and parenting partner and husband Toby live in Cincinnati,

Ohio where they have raised three thriving kids who are now grown—Evy, Mick, and Peter. Renee and Toby love when all their kids are home and under one roof.

Despite her busy life, she regularly carves out quiet time to read, write, and spend time in prayer and loves to take sunrise morning walks and spend time with her closest longtime friends.

Child in Bloom Services

Parents can connect personally with Dr. Renee Mattson through her business, Child in Bloom, which specializes in parental and educational coaching. She provides private coaching and group trainings that focus on differentiated strategies to support improved learning and behavioral outcomes for children of all ages. Additionally, she offers in-home and in-school observational support and guidance for parents and educators.

Businesses, organizations, and churches dedicated to supporting parents often invite Renee to present to both large and small groups in need of parenting assistance.

Her work has positively impacted thousands of parents and educators across the United States.

To learn more about Renee's services, visit www.childinbloom.com.